Exploring the School Leadership Landscape

ALSO AVAILABLE FROM BLOOMSBURY

New Primary Leaders: International Perspectives, Edited by Michael Cowie
School and System Leadership: Changing Roles for Primary Headteachers,
Susan Robinson
Rethinking Educational Leadership: From Improvement to Transformation,
John West-Burnham
Leadership of Place: Stories from Schools in the US, UK and South Africa,
Kathryn Riley

Exploring the School Leadership Landscape

Changing demands, changing realities

PETER EARLEY

B L O O M S B U R Y

LONDON • NEW DELHI • NEW YORK • SYDNEY

Bloomsbury Academic

An imprint of Bloomsbury Publishing Plc

50 Bedford Square	1385 Broadway
London	New York
WC1B 3DP	NY 10018
UK	USA

www.bloomsbury.com

Bloomsbury is a registered trade mark of Bloomsbury Publishing Plc

First published 2013

© Peter Earley, 2013

British Library Cataloguing-in-Publication Data
A catalogue record for this book is available from the British Library.

ISBN: HB: 978-1-4725-0833-1
PB: 978-1-4725-0602-3
ePub: 978-1-4725-0766-2
ePDF: 978-1-4725-0663-4

Library of Congress Cataloging-in-Publication Data
A catalogue record for this book is available from the Library of Congress

Typeset by Newgen Knowledge Works (P) Ltd., Chennai, India
Printed and bound in Great Britain

Contents

Figures and tables

Figures

Tables

Acknowledgements

The author would like to thank all those who helped and contributed to the writing of this book, especially Sara Bubb who edited the first draft and made it more reader-friendly! It is based on a series of studies on school leadership from 2002 to 2012 but draws most heavily on the recent study on the changing school landscape, funded by the National College, undertaken in 2012 with colleagues from the Institute of Education, Rob Higham, Rebecca Allen, Tracey Allen and Rebecca Nelson and the National Foundation for Educational Research, especially Sarah Lynch, Palak Mehta and David Sims. Many thanks to Andy Coleman and the National College for School Leadership for giving permission to allow data (especially tables and figures) and extracts from this report (and others involving the author) to be reproduced. A version of Chapter 2 was first published in *Educational Management, Administration and Leadership* as 'School autonomy and government control: School leaders' views on a changing policy landscape in England' and thanks are offered to Sage Publications for permission to reproduce parts of it here. The author is also grateful to the OECD for permission to reproduce Figure 7.1, taken from Schleicher, A. (ed.) (2012) *Preparing Teachers and Developing School Leaders for the 21st Century: Lessons from around the World*, Paris: OECD Publishing. http://dx.doi.org.

Abbreviations

AST	Advanced Skills Teacher
CPD	Continuing professional development
DCSF	Department for Children, Schools and Families
DfE	Department for Education
EBACC	English Baccalaureate
HEI	Higher education institution
HMI	Her Majesty's Inspectorate
LA	Local authority
LEA	Local education authority
LLE	Local Leader of Education
NCSL	National College for School Leadership
NFER	National Foundation for Educational Research
NLE	National Leader of Education
NLG	National Leader of Governance
NPQH	National Professional Qualification for Headship
NQT	Newly qualified teacher
OECD	Organisation for Economic and Cultural Development
Ofsted	Office for Standards in Education
PwC	PricewaterhouseCoopers
SLE	Specialist Leader of Education
SLT	Senior leadership team
SMT	Senior management team
SQH	Scottish Qualification for Headship
TSA	Teaching School Alliance

Notes on contributors

Peter Earley holds the Chair of Educational Leadership and Management at the London Centre for Leadership in Learning (LCLL) at the Institute of Education, University of London, United Kingdom. Before joining the Institute in the mid 1990s he worked as a school teacher in London, a university lecturer in Australia and on numerous research and evaluation projects at England's National Foundation for Educational Research. Peter's interests are wide-ranging and cover the leadership and governance of schools, leadership development, impact evaluation of professional development, human resource management, and school inspection and evaluation. Peter has published extensively in the field and led many externally funded research projects and consultancies.

Rebecca Allen is a reader in Economics of Education at the Institute of Education, University of London, United Kingdom. Her principal research interests lie within the economics of schooling and effect of government policies on school behaviour and performance. Past research includes studies of school choice, school accountability measures, the role of faith schools in state education and competition between schools. Rebecca is currently working on a quantitative analysis of the teacher labour market, with a particular focus on the early career choices of teachers. For all her research she uses very large-scale datasets combined with quantitative evaluation methods.

Rob Higham is a senior lecturer in the LCLL at the Institute of Education, University of London, United Kingdom. Rob's research has included work on school leadership and improvement, school collaboration and markets in education and educational policy. Rob supported recently the work of the National Audit Office, United Kingdom, on the Academies programme and is currently leading research on new models of schooling, including Free Schools, and on leadership responses to school autonomy policies. Rob also pursues research in South Africa and South Asia, where he was part of a British Academy UK South Asia Partnership with colleagues in the United Kingdom, India and Nepal looking at issues of education and social inequality.

Shenila Rawal is an education economist working at the Institute of Education, University of London, United Kingdom. She is particularly interested in teacher quality and effectiveness, the relationship between poverty and educational outcomes, and the role of gender and social distance in reducing economic and educational gaps internationally. Her research has involved training and experience in applying quantitative evaluation methods to analyse large-scale datasets as well as collecting and analysing primary data. She has worked as an external consultant for several organizations such as the Department for International Development (DFID), Cambridge Education and the World Bank.

1

Setting the Scene

Leadership matters

Numerous studies and reports from researchers, national inspectors and others, claim that leadership is a crucial factor in organizational effectiveness and the key to school success and improvement. In many countries the role of leaders, especially headteachers or principals, in promoting student learning is an important facet of education policy discussions. Strong leadership is viewed as especially important for the regeneration or 'turning round' of failing schools and in enabling schools to achieve excellence or become world class. Over the last decade the discourse about leadership has grown in importance both in the United Kingdom and globally. In November 2000 in England the National College for School Leadership (NCSL) was established. International and National Leadership Centres are now commonplace and reflect the significance policymakers accord to the notion of educational leaders and leadership development. Recent research and inspection reports consistently point to the importance of leadership and the positive effect leaders can have on underachieving schools and student outcomes. For example, the 2012 annual report from Her Majesty's Chief Inspector entitles the first chapter 'the importance of leadership' and notes:

> If England is to compete with the very best, then strong leadership is absolutely critical. *Therefore, this report is fundamentally about the importance of leadership at every level* . . . leaders are the key people in changing and improving the culture and performance of the organisation.

Leaders provide the role models for the rest of the institution. (Ofsted, 2012a, p. 9, original italics)

Wherever organizational success is found, good leadership is said to be behind it. High-quality leadership, at all levels, is therefore one of the key requirements of successful schools and leaders can have a significant positive impact on student outcomes – second only to classroom teaching as a school influence (Leithwood et al., 2004). An attempt to quantify the precise influence that headteachers or principals have on student achievement has been undertaken by Branch et al. (2013) who drew on matched data sets collected over many years by the Texas Schools Project. They found considerable variation in principal effectiveness, noting that 'highly effective principals raise student achievement by between two and seven months of learning in a single school year' (2013, p. 63). They also note that ineffective principals lower student achievement by the same amount. Although the impact is smaller than that associated with highly effective teachers the authors comment that 'teachers have a direct impact on only those students in their classroom; differences in principal quality affect all students in a given school' (ibid., p. 63).

This leadership influence is predominately indirect, in that it relates to influence on the school's organization and the teaching and learning environment, rather than a direct influence on student achievement. Leithwood and Seashore-Louis (2012, p. 3) summarize the consistency of these findings when they state 'to date, we have not found a single documented case of a school improving its student achievement record in the absence of talented leadership'. Effective leadership, potential leaders and their development are crucial to the future success of all educational systems.

Yet despite the emphasis in the policy literature and elsewhere on the key role of effective leaders, particularly headteachers or principals, and the many definitions of leadership that appear in the literature, 'there remains very little consensus concerning what leadership is and what *it comprises* (Kruger and Scheerens, 2012, p. 1, original italics). This book aims to make a contribution to this ongoing debate about leadership and its importance. It is different from most however, in that given the centrality of leadership for effective school performance, it considers critically how school leadership has changed over the first decade of the twenty-first century to meet the ever-growing and changing demands of policymakers and other stakeholders. The constant factor over this time period has been the need to raise standards and continuously improve in an attempt to raise the quality of the student learning experience. This period has been described by Cranston (2013, p. 131) as 'an era of standards-based agendas, enhanced centralized accountability systems where improved student learning, narrowly defined, becomes the mantra for school leaders, who themselves are subject to enhanced accountabilities'.

The research base

This book is research informed. It is based largely around a series of research studies into school leadership published between 2002 and 2012. During that time, four large-scale studies of the general state of school leadership in England have been funded by the NCSL (referred to as the National College [NC]) and the Department for Education (DfE) – those by Earley et al., in 2002; Stevens et al., in 2005; PricewaterhouseCoopers (PwC), in 2007; and finally and most recently, by Earley et al., in 2012. These four research-based reviews of the state of the school leadership landscape in England, published between 2002 and 2012, which used a range of quantitative and qualitative data collection methods, are used throughout the book to act as a benchmark or foundation to consider the changing landscape of schools and the implications for school leaders. The first baseline study was conducted in the early 2000s by the IOE, University of London and published in 2002 soon after the establishment of the NCSL. The follow-up study was conducted by MORI Social Research Institute and published in 2005. The third study, entitled an *Independent Study of School Leadership*, was conducted by a management consultancy firm, PwC, in 2007, whilst the most recent study by the Institute of Education, undertaken in conjunction with the National Foundation for Educational Research, was published in December 2012. Further details of each study are given in Table 1.1.

Therefore the ways in which school leadership and its practice have changed and developed in response to a rapidly changing educational context in England is the central focus of this book. For example, in 2007 the policy landscape was found to have changed considerably over the previous decade 'so that what leaders are expected to do now and in the future is significantly different from what it was even a few years ago' (PwC, 2007, p. v). Something similar could be said today. Throughout the book empirical evidence is drawn upon from a variety of sources, including the above reviews and especially the 2012 landscape study, to consider what has changed but also what has remained largely the same over the ten-year time period of the study.

In the course of the detailed reviews of the evolving school leadership landscape, the work of school leaders, the relation between leadership and student learning, professional learning and leadership for learning, accountability and the market, leadership and governance, leadership distribution, system leadership, and school autonomy and the self-improving system are discussed. The various ways in which school leadership, and headship in

TABLE 1.1 The leadership landscape studies – 2002–12

Report title	Date of publication	Funder	Main forms of data collection	Authors and institution
Establishing the current state of school leadership in England	2002	Department of Education and Skills	Questionnaire surveys Interviews focus groups 10 case studies	Earley, Evans, Collarbone, Gold and Halpin Institute of Education University of London
Follow up Research into the State of School Leadership in England	2005	Department of Education and Skills	Questionnaire surveys Bulletin board/ focus groups	Stevens, Brown, Knibbs and Smith MORI Social Research Institute
Independent Study into School Leadership	2007	Department of Education and Skills	Questionnaire surveys interviews focus groups 50 meetings 50 school visits	No named authors Pricewaterhouse Coopers
Review of the School Leadership Landscape	2012	National College for School Leadership	Questionnaire surveys 50 interviews, 3 focus groups, 8 case studies	Earley, Higham, Allen, R, Allen, T, Howson, Nelson, Rawal (IOE) Lynch, Morton, Mehta and Sims (NFER)

particular, has undergone significant changes especially in the wake of ever-increasing autonomy and devolved responsibility to the school site, are given consideration. As was written in the first baseline study in 2002:

> Schools are now more complex organisations to manage than previously, notably with regard to budgets, human resources, professional development and administration generally. Consequently, there is today much more to manage and to take a lead on, with the result that modern

headteachers and their deputies, and other school leaders, work for long hours . . . probably longer than their predecessors. (Earley et al., 2002, p. 17)

Data from the 2012 landscape study will be drawn upon extensively to consider these and other matters but the book also includes an up-to-date review of relevant literature in a critical but informed manner. In the context of the four school leadership reviews published in 2002, 2005, 2007 and 2012, the main focus is on the decade between the first and last leadership landscape studies – 2002–2012 – enabling the book to contribute originally to debates over leadership effectiveness and leadership in practice. The rapidly changing policy context over this period has brought with it increasing responsibilities and challenges for schools in particular within a framework that seeks to enhance quality of provision and student outcomes within an increasingly autonomous system with a high stakes accountability culture.

Three key conclusions from the leadership reviews are worth noting:

- The growing complexity of school leadership and management. This has been the case particularly from the late 1980s, following the Education Reform Act (ERA), the Local Management of Schools (LMS) and the creation of education markets, which have nearly always led to intensification in the work of school leaders.

- A combination of demographic pressures and a declining pool of middle leaders attracted by headship (given in part workload and accountability pressures) have made the recruitment and retention of headteachers in particular more difficult.

- In part as a response to these challenges, a number of new models of school leadership have been identified. While the traditional model, of a senior leadership team (SLT) composed of a headteacher and deputy and/or assistant heads, was still found to be the most common, new models were noted by the 2007 report, including a managed model; a multi-agency model; a federated model; and a system leadership model.

Despite a substantial evidence base on effective school leadership, research has also questioned whether school leaders can fulfil the tasks recommended by many post-1988 ERA effectiveness studies. In light of these debates, the issues of context, accountability and the quasi-market and their influence on school leaders, including how their combination has led to an intensification and distribution of leadership within schools and an uneasy tension between local leadership and central managerialism are worth noting. These issues are considered further in the concluding chapter along with the changing school landscape as we move into the mid-2010s.

Overview

Although this is a study of schools in England it clearly has wider significance and will be of interest to readers who work, study or research in other educational systems. The book consists of eight chapters and a conclusion. The second chapter, written by Dr Rob Higham the co-director of the 2012 leadership landscape study, examines the current policy landscape as it affects school leaders and leadership and considers how schools are responding. It does so by drawing on data from the 2012 study and presents the views of headteachers, senior/middle leaders and chairs of governors on a range of government policies and their potential impact on schools. Following Chapter 2's brief historical and analytical perspective on school autonomy for the period 2002–12, it notes how school autonomy as well as accountability, school partnerships, external support, the role of the Local Authority (LA), and managing change were key themes in the 2012 research. Empirical data are used to review these themes and the implications for autonomy and control discussed within the wider literature. The balance between autonomy and control, variations in responses between school leaders, and the implications of reform are discussed.

The majority of school leaders involved in the 2012 research generally viewed autonomy positively, but significantly they did not anticipate gaining further autonomy in practice. There appeared to be a clear contrast between the rhetoric and the reality of the school autonomy discourse. The freedom and capacity to act also was found to vary considerably depending on a number of factors but most importantly according to school phase and size. Secondary and larger schools were more able to absorb the greater operational powers (Simkins, 1997) that came with the changing policy landscape. For smaller schools and many primary schools, such additional powers simply made it more difficult for them to keep their focus on learning-centred leadership (Southworth, 2009).

In Chapter 2 a typology of four groups of schools is developed, drawing on statistical analysis of headteacher responses to the rapidly changing educational policy landscape. These groups of schools are labelled as: confident, cautious, concerned and constrained. The latter was found to be the smallest group, where about one-in-eight headteachers viewed policy negatively and were relatively sceptical, even cynical about its intentions and potential impact. The analysis indicates how in 2012 increasing operational power, declining support from LAs and differential regulation of schools has the potential to reproduce and exacerbate local hierarchies of schools which may exist between schools (Waslander et al., 2010). These important themes are further developed in the final chapter.

Chapter 3 on the demography of leadership and the leadership labour market is also written by colleagues from the Institute of Education (IOE). Drs Rebecca Allen and Shenila Rawal draw upon relevant data sets, especially the School Workforce Census of 2010 and November 2011, to analyse the structure of leadership teams and demographic characteristics of school leaders and teachers across different types of state-funded schools in England. The job transitions of school teachers and leaders, their age, sex, ethnic and subject background, differences in tenure, hours spent teaching, promotion rates and choices of school are analysed and comparisons made, where data permit, with the situation previously found. The analysis of the changing school leadership demography and the labour market highlights three key observations.

- Although teaching clearly continues to be a female-dominated profession, it is striking the extent to which smaller proportions of women than men moved into each stage of senior leadership. The census data show that male teachers were more likely to make long-distance (i.e. regional) geographic job moves in order to achieve promotion and that female teachers choose to make far greater use of internal promotions at their existing school.

- The teacher labour market is segmented with relatively little movement between geographic regions or even between school governance types. Voluntary-aided schools displayed the highest likelihood of employing teachers who have previously worked within their sector. Senior leadership posts are far more segmented both regionally and by governance than classroom teacher posts and senior leaders became increasingly constrained geographically by family and other considerations, compared to the relatively younger pool of classroom teachers.

- The issue of deputy head turnover is important. The data suggest a reduction of such posts and little turnover and thus a degree of 'blocking' promotional opportunities. Turnover of such posts is important to ensure a pool of applicants for headship going forward to prevent possible future shortages, particularly important during a period of succession planning challenges and changes to the policy landscape. Currently about 1500 heads retire each year (about 7% of schools).

Chapter 4 considers two aspects of the changing leadership landscape. First it describes models of leadership and school organization and how these have changed or not. It is interesting to note that despite many changes over ten years, especially in relation to school structures, in 2012 the sole headteacher of a single school working with a single governing body was still the dominant model. Examples were found of other arrangements but they were the exception and not the rule. Different models and organizational arrangements and how they have changed over time are discussed with reference to future trends and developments as schools are encouraged to move towards a self-improving system. Leadership approaches, recruitment and retention and the levels of involvement in leadership tasks and activities by various members of the school community are also discussed. The second part of the chapter considers the most significant challenges faced by school leaders and compares these challenges with those mentioned in earlier studies. The main concern in the 2012 study was financial, with four out of ten headteachers, one-third of governors and a quarter of senior/middle leaders anticipating finance/budget issues and reductions in funding due to the government's austerity measures.

Given the policy changes over the period of the four leadership studies, the role of school governance is of increasing significance and is the focus of Chapter 5. The governing body represents an important element of school leadership; it is the strategic, accountable body for the school. Governing bodies' role in school improvement has increased in importance. Current policy change, especially the adoption of academy status, is adding new complexity to the governor role, with governors having to keep abreast of policy and other matters affecting the strategic direction of their school. Research suggests that the quality of the governing body is an important influence on school improvement: the chair of the governing body needs to be able to negotiate and manage a productive as well as challenging stance with the headteacher. However, evidence suggests that the governor role tends towards scrutiny activity rather than a sustained focus and appraisal of improvement and effectiveness in schools (Ranson, 2008; James, 2011). Certainly an ineffective governing body does appear to have a demonstrable negative impact on outcomes; particularly where there are low levels of governor capacity and competence (Ofsted, 2011a). The chapter draws upon data from the leadership baseline study of 2002 and the landscape study of 2012 to see the extent of governors' involvement in leadership activities and how things have changed or remained the same over time. It also provides information about the composition of school governing bodies, their leadership role, their training and development needs and their views on the educational policy landscape.

A key challenge to heads and other senior leaders in schools is achieving a balance across their various areas of responsibility and ensuring that they focus their time and attention on the things that matter most. This is the central focus of Chapter 6. Keeping their focus on strategic and learning-centred leadership is a continuing challenge. In this chapter the tasks of leaders and their use of time is considered. How has the situation changed, if at all, since the first baseline study in the early 2000s? How this time use compares with heads' ideal use, especially as it relates to strategic, entrepreneurial activities and leading teaching and learning, is also discussed drawing upon the findings of the most recent 2012 landscape study.

How school leaders work to improve teaching and learning is the key focus of the next chapter, which draws upon various data sets, including the Organisation for Economic and Cultural Development's (OECD's), to address questions about the nature of learning-centred leadership and its enactment in the United Kingdom and other countries. In Chapter 7 a theory of learning-centred leadership is outlined and, drawing on the 2012 study, the most important actions being taken by school leaders to lead the improvement of teaching and learning are noted. Research is drawn upon to show how school leaders operate to enhance the quality of teaching and learning and case studies of heads are provided of how leaders attempt to work in a learning-centred manner.

The penultimate chapter draws upon the various research studies to consider preparation for headship, the first year in post, leadership training and development, and perceptions of necessary future leadership skills and qualities. It looks at the extent to which the skills, capabilities, development needs and support required to lead schools successfully have changed over the past decade or so. It discusses leadership development provision and what is perceived as effective leadership preparation, development and training. Consideration is also given to the development and training needs of school leaders, how they are currently being met and how they might be met in the future.

Finally, Chapter 9 looks to the future challenges of leadership and suggests that the complexity of school leadership, and headship in particular, continues to increase with a consequent intensification of work. The need to develop internal school capacity and effective partnerships appear essential for schools as they navigate numerous national policy changes, within their particular contexts. There is a substantial risk however that the nature and demands of current policy change will disrupt the focus of schools and leaders from teaching and learning and their authentic improvement. The landscape is also uneven and there are signs that potential fault lines could be emerging between leaders across school phases, contexts and inspection outcomes.

These fault lines include not only school capacity, but also the ways in which school leaders view the potential impacts of and respond to new policies. The chapter deals with several interrelated issues that are likely to impact on the future of leaders and leadership: the intensification of leadership roles and the importance of distributed leadership; support for schools and the role of the middle tier; the move towards a self-improving school system; leading the learning; and the importance of leadership development for the future. It notes the need to ensure that in an increasingly devolved system adequate resources continue to be devoted to the support and development of school leaders and concludes on both a positive and negative note. Optimism is key but can indeed be hard in a constantly changing educational landscape.

The book aims to explore the changing school leadership landscape giving consideration to the changing demands and changing realities of leadership, especially headship. The next chapter begins this exploration by providing insights into how the policy landscape has changed during the period of study 2002 to 2012.

2

School Autonomy, Government Control and a Changing Policy Landscape

Rob Higham

This chapter explores how school leaders perceive 'school autonomy' and government control, as it exists within the wider policy framework. First, it develops a historical and analytical perspective on school autonomy, especially over the period of the various leadership studies noted in the preceding chapter and after the introduction of the 1988 Education Reform Act (ERA). Second, the 2012 leadership landscape study, involving a survey of almost 2000 school leaders, as well as case study data, are drawn upon to explore the views of school leaders on six interrelated aspects of policy: school autonomy; accountability; partnerships; external support; the Local Authority (LA); and managing change. Third, the chapter considers the implications for debates on school autonomy and central control. Drawing on Simkins' (1997) concepts of operational and criteria power, school leaders are shown to commonly anticipate greater power over aspects of school management but not over the aims and purposes of schooling. A significant variation is also found between school leaders in their perceived capacity and freedom to act. This leads to a proposed typology of four schools: confident, cautious, concerned and constrained. A key implication, the chapter concludes, is that increasing operational power for schools, declining LA support and differentiated school autonomy have the very real potential to exacerbate existing local hierarchies between schools.

Introduction

Over the period of this book's study, 2002–12, there has been a range of debate about school autonomy and accountability measures. The coalition government, elected in May 2010, continued this trend by arguing it would place school autonomy at the centre of its education policy. In the White Paper, *The Importance of Teaching*, the Department for Education (DfE, 2010a, p. 11) argued that:

> Across the world, the case for the benefits of school autonomy has been established beyond doubt. In a school system with good quality teachers, flexibility in the curriculum and clearly established accountability measures, it makes sense to devolve as much day-to-day decision-making as possible to the front line.

Detailing the new forms of autonomy that schools in England could expect the White Paper set out several intentions. First, the removal of 'unnecessary duties and burdens' (DfE, 2010a, p. 12) including reductions in the length of codes and guidance, for instance, on the National Curriculum. Second, the provision of 'greater freedoms to reward good performance and address poor performance' (ibid., p. 25) including new flexibilities on staff pay and conditions and simplified capability procedures. Third, the opportunity for all schools to 'achieve Academy status' (ibid., p. 11), including by extending existing policy on 'transforming' the 'lowest performing schools' into sponsored academies and, perhaps most significantly, by allowing all schools to apply for the right to convert voluntarily to academy status and hence to opt out of LA governance.

The academisation programme commenced under the New Labour government in 2000 with private sponsors leading the governance of new academies usually in areas of high deprivation. Numbers grew gradually over the decade yet in the two years following the White Paper, the number of academies has increased rapidly. In August 2010 there were 203 academies. By March 2013 there were 2,724, the majority of which were secondary schools that had applied to become converter academies. Championing these changes, the secretary of state for education, argued school autonomy was manifestly what school leaders want. Speaking to FASNA (the Freedom and Autonomy for Schools – National Association, which grew out of the

Association of Head Teachers of Grant Maintained Schools), Michael Gove (2012, p. 3) argued:

> We know – from the subsequent embrace of academy freedoms by more than half the nation's secondary heads – that the attractions of autonomy are now clear to leaders responsible for educating more than half the nation's children . . . [G]reater freedom and autonomy for school leaders is the route to genuine and lasting school reform.

Autonomy and control

Glatter (2012) has reviewed the 'rise and rise' of school autonomy in English education policy. With roots in the 1960s, the rise began during the 1970s when critiques of progressive teaching methods and concerns for standards combined, under Thatcherism, with growing hostility towards the perceived excessive control of schools by Local Educational Authorities (LEAs). These critiques reflected the wider rise of neo-liberalism and politically a New Right committed to choice, diversity and competition. The New Right drew closely on New Public Management theory to advocate the creation of markets within public services and the import of business style efficiency and entrepreneurialism (Ball, 2011).

Reflecting these influences, the ERA of 1988 developed a substantially new policy framework for schools (Whitty, 2008). Local Management of Schools, an idea first piloted in a few select local authorities in the early 1980s, gave schools control over their own budgets and daily management, devolving 85 per cent of the LEA budget to schools. Grant Maintained (GM) status enabled schools, following a parental ballot in favour, to opt out of LEA governance and receive their funding directly from central government. Open enrolment enabled schools to admit as many students as they could attract, subject to their physical capacity. This also linked funding more closely to pupil numbers, thereby placing schools in potential competition with one another. A National Curriculum detailed the curriculum content schools should teach and national tests prescribed the nature of summative assessment and the publication of subsequent results. The 1992 Education Act developed a national framework for regular inspections of schools under the Office for Standards in Education (Ofsted).

Following ERA a range of reform has taken place, often at a persistent and rapid pace, but as Glatter (2012, p. 563) argues the 'continuities have been more pronounced than the discontinuities'. The New Labour government elected in 1997 incentivized certain forms of cooperation to balance competition between schools (Higham et al., 2009), but most of the principles of ERA remained central to contemporary policy. Indeed, prime ministerial commitment to the concept of autonomous state schools has notably strengthened. As Whitty (1997, p. 8) details, having introduced GM status, Thatcher 'expressed hope that most schools would eventually opt-out of their LEA to become grant maintained schools'. John Major, who succeeded her as prime minister, 'advanced the idea of introducing legislation to make all schools grant maintained' (ibid., p. 8). Prime Minister Tony Blair (2005, p. 1), having introduced academy status, argued New Labour must 'complete the reforms we began so that in time we have a system of independent, self-governing state schools'. David Cameron, the prime minister at the time of writing, has drawn explicitly on this legacy.

Yet, amid this political consensus, Glatter (2012, p. 564) suggests there is a paradox: 'Despite the persistent and growing emphasis on autonomy most school practitioners consider themselves constrained by government requirements to an extent that is undoubtedly far greater than their forbearers in 1975'. At least three elements of ERA appear to have contributed to this paradox. First, the nature of school autonomy, which from 1988 focused on the delegation of financial and site management and aspects of deregulation, while the traditional fields of professional autonomy, including curriculum and assessment, were prescribed through the National Curriculum and tests. Second, the nature of accountability, which included from 1992 national inspections and published tests, but which subsequently expanded, to include central target setting, intervention and oversight underpinned by government analysis of pupil level data (Ozga, 2009). Third, the operation of the quasi-market, which created incentives for schools to respond to competitive pressures to attract (particular types of) students and which, while varying locally, has further intensified the significance of external accountability judgments and resultant league tables.

In these ways, England has mirrored a wider international trend for enhanced school autonomy to be accompanied by new forms of state control. As Helgoy et al. (2007, p. 198) argue, this trend includes both strong accountability and 're-regulation' where the 'centre reclaims control, often in an indirect manner, through target setting, performance measurement and the use of quality indicators'. As this occurs, however, states have often continued to emphasize aspects of policy that focus on decentralization and autonomy. As such, autonomy can become a relatively 'ambiguous and subtle concept' (Glatter, 2012) about which clear-cut decisions can be hard to uphold (Helgoy et al., 2007).

Autonomy and leadership

In light of these complexities of autonomy and control, the implications for school leaders of the post-ERA policy framework are debated. Many commentators note that, as a result of the simultaneous centralization and decentralization that followed ERA, school leaders have had to manage the competing pressures of local governance, parental choice and central control, in what Simkins (1997) terms a 'balancing act'. There have also been well-documented increases in the workload of school leaders. In the first baseline study (Earley et al., 2002), for instance, it was found schools post-ERA had become more complex to manage, especially in terms of budgets, human resources, professional development and administration, and this had led to longer working hours (see also Chapter 6). Partly for these reasons, however, the importance afforded to leadership, in particular by government, has been seen to increase (Bush, 2008), with a premium placed on 'effective leadership' and knowledge about it. Certainly, for Caldwell and Spinks (1992, p. 22) – early proponents of 'self-managing schools' – 'leadership is central to achieving success under these conditions'.

Despite this rise in the language of leadership however, and not withstanding the substantial evidence base on effective school leadership (e.g. Day et al., 2009; Robinson et al., 2009), a growing body of research has questioned whether school leaders commonly are or can fulfil the tasks recommended by many post-ERA effectiveness studies. Fink (2010), for instance, argues there is a contradiction between the requirement for leaders to be visionary, creative and entrepreneurial and the policy realities they live with, which encourage leadership that is reactive, compliant and managerial. Forrester and Gunter (2009) question whether school leaders have autonomy to develop their own practices or are in fact 'local implementers of reform'. School leaders, they argue, are not naïve readers of policy, and have their own histories, values and interests, but the combination of market forces, accountability and associated central government policy has often constrained local possibilities for thinking and action. School leaders may talk the language of vision but the space in which they can lead may be narrow and in many cases be, as Hartley (2007) argues, tactical interpretation rather than actual strategizing. Lewis and Murphy (2008, pp. 135–6) argue much of the school leadership literature seems to:

> assume that the headteacher is in charge of the school's destiny . . . Yet the reality is that, in some respects, many headteachers are more like branch managers than CEOs. They are handed down expectations, targets, new initiatives and resources – all of which may or may not be manageable in their context.

Considering this balance of autonomy and control from the perspective of power, Simkins (1997) differentiates between criteria and operational power. Criteria power concerns the definition of the aims and purposes of a service (what Simkins terms the 'why and what'). Operational power concerns decisions over how the service is to be provided and resourced (termed the 'how'). For Simkins, while the operational power of school leaders and governors increased significantly following ERA, criteria power was drawn much more firmly into central government and away from LEAs and the teaching profession. In this way, Simkins (1997, p. 22) argues, the resulting domains of autonomy for school leaders 'lie partly at the edges of the "what" – determining aspects of the character of the school . . . but primarily with the "how" of school management: the organization of school'.

Importantly, the extent to which school leaders draw upon this limited criteria power – or 'autonomy around the edges' – may vary between schools. Russell et al. (1997, p. 248) argue this variation depends on how leaders interpret policy – that is, whether they see a specific policy as a 'a strait-jacket, or set of constraints which nevertheless leave considerable opportunities for the exercise of creativ[ity]'. Bush (2008, p. 277) suggests there is also a values dimension, where leaders may have more freedom to pursue their own values where these are consistent with those of government. If they are not, leaders acting autonomously risk censure by, in particular, the inspection agency Ofsted. For Gewirtz (2002, p. 48) the responses of school leaders to policy are influenced by a range of contextual factors, including the market position of their institution and the professional histories of key institutional players.

Gold et al. (2003), drawing on the ten case studies from the first baseline study (Earley et al., 2002), used the term 'principled principals' to describe how highly effective heads were driven by personal, moral and educational values and able to articulate these convincingly creating a clear sense of institutional purpose and direction. They had a passion for the job and mediated externally driven directives to ensure, where possible, they were consistent with what the school was trying to achieve.

Across these potential influences, Hoyle and Wallace (2007) argue the English school system can be characterized by three main types of leadership response to policy. First, leaders who are committed to implementing external direction. Second, leaders who are uncommitted to external managerialism and who manifest this in minimal compliance. Third, leaders who fashion their own commitment to policy while maintaining a steadfast focus on pupil interests. The latter group, Hoyle and Wallace argue, display principled infidelity – that is, they are principled by adapting policy to the needs of students, while also creating the appearance externally that policy is being implemented with fidelity.

Researching the views of school leaders

In the context of these perspectives on school leadership in the post-ERA era, the 2012 leadership landscape study is drawn on to investigate how school leaders view contemporary policy change and how they are planning to respond to it. The other studies which form the basis of this book – Earley et al. (2002), Stevens et al. (2005) and the PricewaterhouseCoopers' (PwC's) (2007) *Independent Study into School Leadership* all looked at the changing policy landscape of schools but did not directly collect evidence of school leaders' views on this as was done in the 2012 study. For example, the 2007 report noted the changing schools' landscape in the mid-2000s included the 'new relationship with schools' (a light touch accountability and self-evaluation system), personalized learning, Every Child Matters (a wide-ranging learning and social agenda for children and young people), partnership working and new learning environments associated with 'Building Schools for the Future'. The 2007 report notes:

> Schools are changing on a number of educational, vocational, social, technological and environmental dimensions. These dimensions will have implications for both the roles and responsibilities of school leaders and for the ways in which schools interact with other educational institutions and external agencies. For example, the remit of schools is expanding as they become increasingly responsible for the delivery of solutions to issues such as social cohesion, citizenship and childhood obesity. (PwC, p. 2)

For many observers of the English education system, contemporary policy is still undergoing a period of rapid change (Baker, 2010). For instance, on school governance, since the publication of the 2007 leadership report there has been a rapid increase in academies, through both central intervention and most numerously voluntary conversion. On accountability, the Ofsted inspection framework, against which schools are judged, has been reformed, with plans also for examination and National Curriculum reforms (Glatter, 2012). On local strategic leadership, the role of local authorities is changing in response to both an increase in self-governing academies and significant central funding cuts (Hastings et al., 2012). On wider support for schools, a number of national agencies have been closed, with government support instead for a school improvement market and a Teaching Schools agenda (Smith, 2012). The government has argued its reforms will increase the autonomy of schools. Given the complexities that exist, however, in the balance between autonomy and control, the 2012 landscape study has sought to understand how school leaders perceive school autonomy, as it exists within the wider policy framework.

Autonomy and the current policy framework

Six themes emerged as being of particular importance. These were: school autonomy; accountability; school partnerships; external support; the changing role of the LA; and managing change. These themes are now considered in detail. In the subsequent section, the implications for debates over autonomy and control are discussed.

School autonomy

Survey respondents were asked about their views on school autonomy in general and about gaining academy status in practice. On school autonomy in general, three broad perspectives emerged. First, half of headteachers were positive about the potential impact of their school becoming more independent and autonomous but a third were negative. Second, headteachers and governors held similar perspectives on the potential use by schools of greater autonomy. Half of both groups felt greater autonomy would enable their school to improve teaching and learning and to use financial resources better to support school priorities (while less than a quarter disagreed). Third, however, despite current policy statements, over half of headteachers (56%) did not think their institution would actually gain more autonomy in practice but a quarter thought they would.

There were significant differences on these matters among headteachers. By school type, an overwhelming majority of academy principals (97%) were positive about school autonomy in general, while among community school headteachers exactly one-half were positive but over a third (36%) were negative. By school phase, a majority of secondary school headteachers (68%) was positive about school autonomy in general, while among primary headteachers one-half (49%) were positive but about a third (37%) were negative.

On becoming an academy in practice, 10 per cent of schools had already or were currently transferring to academy status, 8 per cent were planning to become an academy and 79 per cent had no plans to do so. These proportions were in keeping with the national proportion of schools that were academies at the time of the survey sample creation in November 2011. A significant phase difference was again apparent, while 56 per cent of secondary schools had already become or had plans to become an academy, this was only true for 12 per cent of primary schools.

A number of motivations emerged for not converting to academy status, particularly among primary schools. First, several headteachers reported their school was already relatively independent and had gained new autonomies over procurement as LA service provision declined. One headteacher summarized, 'more autonomy is not a big issue for us'. Second, several headteachers were not certain that academy status would secure additional resources for their school and also noted their LA provided, as one headteacher described, 'protection if things went wrong – which they can sometimes do'. Not wanting to lose this support, they were happy for others to 'test the water'. Third, a number of school leaders were concerned that a direct relationship with government could lead to greater oversight or intervention. As one chair of governors argued:

> Autonomy is good . . . but centralizing could be just as dangerous. We would rather seek to protect our school community. We may not be seen to be outstanding by a centralized gaze.

School leaders that had already or were contemplating converting to academy status also discussed a number of motivations for doing so, particularly among secondary schools. First, several school leaders had converted to academy status to 'stay the same'. They did not anticipate making changes to teaching and learning or pay and conditions and decided to become an academy in the face of external change. Second, not all schools converted to academy status from a position of strength. Several had chosen to become an academy in partnership with another school to avoid potential forms of intervention, including sponsored academisation. As one headteacher described, this was to 'take charge of one's own destiny'. Third, several other school leaders said they had contemplated conversion to support other schools. One primary academy principal, for example, described plans for an academy trust were 'to provide a local solution for other schools . . . [so they] did not get hoovered up by a local secondary, or a chain'.

Academies, and schools becoming academies, also commonly referred to the financial incentives of conversion. The Association of School and College Leaders reported from a 2011 survey of 1,471 secondary schools that 72 per cent of respondents saw financial gain as a reason for pursuing academy status (Mansell, 2011). Among the case study and interview participants these incentives were clearest among two groups. First, 'early converters', that calculated the additional funding schools received on conversion, the Local Authority Central Spend Equivalent Grant (LACSEG), was initially on the generous side. Second, 'net beneficiaries' that did not regularly use LA improvement services and calculated LACSEG funding would be greater than the additional costs of academy status, such as financial management or pension contributions. A third group, of more recent converters, expressed concern about being 'left behind' in an LA system with declining funds. In these ways, rather than autonomy per se, a majority of schools converting to academy status expressed contextual and financial influences for doing so. For most, autonomy was not a primary driver and often appeared imprecise or uncertain.

School accountability

These views related closely to accountability and perceived external limits to autonomy. Accountability was seen to be a necessary part of a public education system, but school leaders expressed concerns about the current framework. These were reflected in challenges school leaders reported (see also Chapter 4). The most common challenge was reductions in funding followed by the new Ofsted inspection framework. Academy status and sustaining/improving student outcomes (particularly attainment) were also noted as concerns. Notably, less than 10 per cent of each group identified directly improving the quality of teaching and learning.

Senior leaders were also asked in the 2012 survey about specific aspects of accountability. On inspection, over two-fifths (43%) of headteachers and senior/middle leaders reported the new Ofsted inspection framework would have a negative impact on their school. Interview and case study participants in the 2012 research, while expressing support for a focus on teaching and learning in the new framework, commonly felt recent inspections had become a more negative experience and 'punitive', with inspectors seeking to identify faults rather than working with schools to identify areas for improvement. Schools seeking to improve from a 'satisfactory' grading (now known as 'requires improvement') were more likely to respond in this way; school leaders commonly perceived their autonomy was being constrained increasingly by Ofsted.

On the planned National Curriculum review, school leaders were mixed about its potential impacts, with senior/middle leaders more positive (56%) than headteachers. The potential of greater curriculum autonomy had been weakened significantly by accountability changes. This was particularly the case for secondary headteachers who were commonly negative about the mid-year introduction of the English Baccalaureate (EBACC) and about the implications for vocational subjects and wider conceptions of learning.

School leaders were more neutral towards accountability to parent choice, with about 56 per cent of heads, governors and senior/middle leaders suggesting that current reform neither further encouraged nor discouraged competition with other schools. Among case study participants, incentives for competition were most clearly observed in contexts of demographic declines, surplus places and/or funding pressures. This included secondary schools managing the interim between a small current age cohort of students and larger cohorts entering local nurseries.

Collaboration with other schools

Notwithstanding evidence of highly competitive local contexts, the majority of school leaders were positive about school-to-school collaboration. Over 80 per cent agreed that working in partnership with other schools was critical to improving outcomes for students. Approximately 60 per cent also felt the current policy agenda encouraged their school to form collaborative partnerships with other schools. About half of headteachers and chairs of governors felt encouraged to formally support another school's improvement.

Interview and case study participants were also mainly positive about the potential of partnership working. A widely held view was that schools, including academies, needed to be conceived locally as interdependent rather than independently autonomous. They also noted, however, a range of local obstacles to realizing collaboration. While several schools reported the benefits of supportive local relations, others faced local distrust that reduced their ability to contribute to and gain from rigorous collaboration. The movement of schools to academy status was also seen to have the potential to change local dynamics of trust, particularly where new academies had given less priority to existing partnerships, for instance, on exclusions. Schools previously in receipt of initiative funding, such as Behaviour Improvement Partnerships and Excellence Clusters, had also experienced a reduction in funding that had supported collaboration.

School leaders also noted the potential of new sponsored partnerships to reinforce existing local hierarchies. There was a perception among schools judged not to be 'outstanding' or schools with lower levels of student attainment that the Teaching School agenda was for schools with 'higher status'. This had ramifications for which schools would benefit most. Perhaps most importantly, schools recognizing they might have most to gain from collaborative working were not always well placed to engage with such work. For some, a vulnerability to external intervention had led to wariness about collaboration given uncertainty over whether partnerships might become new forms of intervention. For others there was a range of perceived time, capacity and accountability constraints. One headteacher, for example, reflected that:

> There are some schools locally it would be very useful for us to work in partnership with, but it's a conflict, because we need to do that, but because of all the pressures, you don't have the time to get into that as much as we would like. It's a frustration.

External support

Headteachers were asked about the external support they accessed more widely. They were asked to indicate: which sources of external support and advice they currently accessed; which three sources they currently considered most important; and which three sources they anticipated to be the most important in 18 months' time. The results are shown in Table 2.1. The LA (54%), the School Improvement Partner (SIP, which is no longer statutory) (52%) and informal support from another state school (31%) were most commonly reported to be one of their three most important current sources of support. Notably, however, it was among these three sources that headteachers anticipated a decline in support over the next 18 months, particularly the LA and SIP. Overall, the anticipated level of decline (−51% points) was broadly similar to the increases in support anticipated elsewhere (+43% points). The anticipated increase, however, was spread across a wide range of providers, many of which were not currently used by most schools. These included commercial organizations, Teaching Schools, National and Local Leaders of Education and the central services of a chain.

TABLE 2.1 Current and future sources of external support among headteachers, 2012

	Current sources of support (tick all that apply) (%)	Three most important sources now (tick only 3) (%)	Three most important in 18 months (tick only 3) (%)	Change in three most important sources (% points)
Local Authority	87	54	29	−25
School Improvement Partner	77	52	32	−20
Informal support from another school	56	37	31	−6
Professional Association/ Union	56	23	23	0
National College for School Leadership	46	19	19	0

	Current sources of support (tick all that apply) (%)	Three most important sources now (tick only 3) (%)	Three most important in 18 months (tick only 3) (%)	Change in three most important sources (% points)
Ofsted	35	13	15	+2
A private consultant or small consultancy	28	19	20	+1
Diocese Board or Chain	28	13	13	0
Schools Forum	22	7	7	0
Commercial organization	19	9	15	+6
Specialist Schools and Academies Trust	15	6	11	+5
National or Local Leader of Education	11	6	14	+8
Teaching School	8	4	13	+9
Central services of a school chain	3	2	7	+5
Specialist Leader in Education	2	1	5	+4
Other	8	7	7	0
No response	2	5	8	-
N -	833	827	826	-

Note: More than one answer could be put forward so percentages may sum to more than 100.
Source: Earley et al., 2012, p. 97.

These trends in support were consistent with the actions headteachers reported undertaking at a whole school level. On LA services, 41 per cent of headteachers had stopped or intended to stop using some of the services provided by their LA. A majority of schools (69%), however, reported they were already or planned to collaborate with other schools to fund aspects of the LA to ensure specific services were sustained. Indeed, for many, external changes to the LA and its capacity to continue to deliver services, rather than the purposefully use of school autonomy in procurement, appeared to be a significant driver of change, particularly where school relations with the LA were historically strong.

The changing role of the LA

External changes to the role of LAs have several contemporary sources. These include the growth in schools leaving LA governance through academisation, with LAs also losing the funding delegated to academies (under LACSEG). Local government has also faced significant funding cuts, more generally, estimated by Hastings et al. (2012) to equate to a 40 per cent decrease in grants from central government between 2011/12 and 2014/15. While these reductions have not been distributed equally, with LAs in urban and poorer parts of England facing the largest decreases (Crawford and Phillips, 2012), a majority of LAs have needed to reduce expenditure by making cuts to the services they offer (Hastings et al., 2012). By May 2011, for instance, a BBC/CIPFA survey found that 26 per cent of LAs had already made reductions to their School Improvement Services (the second most common cut to children's services after youth services) (ibid.).

In the 2012 landscape study, nearly three-quarters (73%) of senior/middle leaders and governors and exactly two-thirds of headteachers reported that current changes to the role of their LA would impact negatively on their school. Within this overall perspective there were significant differences. While the majority of academy principals (71%) were positive about their LA's changing role, only a quarter of community school headteachers were positive and 71 per cent were negative. Also, while 41 per cent of secondary school headteachers were positive and 49 per cent were negative, among primary headteachers only 23 per cent were positive and 72 per cent were negative.

Many participants reported the influence of their LA was in some form of decline. This included contexts where specific school services had already been discontinued or where schools perceived fewer LA officers were trying to cover a range of previous roles, without the relevant expertise, experience or time to do so. For schools that perceived these changes negatively, there were also clear implications for the practice of school leadership. As one headteacher argued:

> I personally don't like the way the LA has almost faded into the background and we are supposed or expected to do everything. That's fine if you're a head and a manager [of a larger school], and your only job is managing the school. But when you've got a massive teaching commitment, trying to find time to go through service agreements, health and safety, maintenance and the building and all the other things – to be honest it's utterly ludicrous.

Managing policy change

In the context of this wide range of reform since the coalition government's election in 2010, school leaders were asked about managing change. Over 80 per cent of senior leaders and chairs of governors reported their school had the confidence to manage current policy change. There was a range of views, however, on the aims and potential impact of policy. While a third of headteachers, for instance, agreed they felt able to work with current policy to support their school's aims and values, another third disagreed. Similarly, while 20 per cent of headteachers agreed their pupils would benefit from current policy reforms, 41 per cent disagreed.

In light of these differences, further statistical analysis (a Latent Class Analysis) was undertaken to provide an overarching analysis of how headteachers understand and plan to respond to current policy changes. By searching for key patterns across responses, underlying types of similar individuals (known as latent classes) can be revealed. Four latent classes of headteacher respondents were identified and defined thematically. Table 2.2 sets out the size and thematic definitions for each class or category.

The association between each class or category and school background characteristics was analysed. No statistically significant relationship was identified between the classes and free school meal (FSM) bands. There was however a statistical likelihood of: Academy principals and headteachers of 'outstanding' secondary schools being located in Class 1; 'Good' schools, in both primary and secondary phases, being located in Class 2 and Class 3; Primary, community and voluntary controlled schools, as compared to foundation schools and academies, being located in Class 4. The categorizations are briefly explained in the next section.

TABLE 2.2 Four categories or classes

Classes	N	%	Thematic definition	Categorization
Class 1	183	22	Positive about school autonomy and confident about actively pursuing new policy opportunities	Confident
Class 2	286	34	Moderately positive about school autonomy, but cautious about engaging with policy	Cautious
Class 3	264	32	Apprehensive about school autonomy and concerned about the potential impacts of policy	Concerned
Class 4	100	12	Neutral on school autonomy, but sceptical about the aims and constraints of policy and negative about the potential impacts	Constrained or cynical

Source: Adapted from Earley et al., 2012, p. 63.

Confident

These headteachers were found to be confident and positive about school autonomy in general (89%), with a majority perceiving they would gain new autonomies in practice (58%). They felt able to work with policy to support their school's aims and values (76%) and believed their students would benefit from current policy (69%). They welcomed the changing role of the LA (71%) and were commonly planning to or already pursuing new policy opportunities, including by becoming an academy (56%), a Teaching School (22%) or part of a Teaching School Alliance (TSA) (50%).

Cautious

These headteachers were moderately positive about school autonomy (58%). They were uncertain (78%), however, about whether schools would gain more autonomy and 88 per cent did not currently plan to become an academy. They were negative about the changing role of the LA (72%) and, while being moderately positive about policy on Teaching Schools, the majority did not currently plan to become a Teaching School (91%) or part of a TSA (77%).

Concerned

These headteachers were concerned about school autonomy. Over half (56%) felt greater autonomy would impact negatively on their school and the vast majority (92%) did not plan to become an academy. They were concerned about the changing role of the LA (83%). Half saw incentives in policy for partnership working, although exactly three-quarters did not plan to join a TSA. Two-thirds saw 'very little' incentives in policy for school improvement (67%) (rather than none at all).

Constrained or cynical

These headteachers were negative about policy and sceptical about its aims. They were mixed in their perspectives on school autonomy, but did not plan to become an academy (92%) and felt the changing role of the LA would impact negatively on their school (86%). The majority reported policy did not ('not at all') provide an incentive to improve pupil achievement (84%) or to focus leadership on teaching and learning (83%).

Wider implications

In exploring how school leaders view contemporary policy change and how they are planning to respond to it, this chapter has considered a variety of perspectives on school autonomy and how autonomy is influenced by accountability, central control and local support and collaboration. Three themes are now discussed that both summarize the main areas of consensus and disagreement among school leaders and point to the wider implications. These are: the balance between autonomy and control; variations between school leaders; and the implications of reform.

Autonomy and control

First, on the balance between autonomy and control, the views of a majority of school leaders related closely to the conceptualization proposed by Simkins (1997) of criteria and operational power. Simkins argued operational power – over how the school is organized – was increased for school leaders in 1988 under ERA, while criteria power – over the aims and purposes of schools – was simultaneously centralized. In 2012, a majority of the survey respondents reported the continuation of these two trends.

On operational power, schools noted the further delegation of managerial power and responsibilities, many of which were at the expense of the LA, extended the trajectory of ERA. Academy status, in particular, was seen to create additional spheres for schools to manage, including financial and site management, pay and conditions and the procurement of services and support. Importantly, however, it was not only academies that reported change, but also schools in contexts of LA decline where greater operational power was being delegated in part by default rather than by intent or design of schools.

On criteria power, school leaders commonly considered the aims and purposes of schooling to remain tightly held by central government. Contemporary change was seen to include refinements to the ERA policy framework, but in a way that sustained government control including through the definition of standards, inspections and intervention. In fields where government claimed new autonomies for schools, for instance over aspects of the curriculum and assessment, many schools reported further refinements to central control, for instance through new definitions of measures of success. Partly for these reasons, while a majority of school leaders viewed autonomy in general positively, they did not anticipate gaining further autonomy in practice.

Variations between school leaders

Within this overarching perspective on the balance between autonomy and control, the second theme for discussion concerns variations in experience and practice between school leaders. Russell et al. (1997) have discussed the existence of different interpretations of policy among school leaders. Hoyle and Wallace (2005) explored different responses to policy and Ball et al. (2012) detailed the complex influences of context on policy enactment. The 2012 survey data suggests two further related aspects are also of importance to differentiation among school leaders. These concern specifically 'who has autonomy' (Cribb and Gewirtz, 2007), where autonomy is understood as the freedom and capacity to act (Lundquist, 1987; Helgoy et al., 2007).

On the capacity to act, differentiation among respondents related most clearly to school phase. Secondary school leaders were more likely to be positive about academy status and the changing role of the LA. Primary school leaders were commonly negative. This may relate, in part, to a longer experience of independence from the LA among secondary schools. Certainly, larger schools appeared more able to absorb additional operational power. For smaller schools, new roles and duties were more likely to be seen to have the potential to disrupt a focus on teaching and learning. Rather than phase per se, however, this also reflected wider variations in the capacity of schools to manage increased operational power. For stand-alone schools vulnerable to LA decline, additional autonomy over finance, human resources and the procurement of services could appear as unwanted burdens.

On the freedom to act, the statistical analysis identified an association between headteacher views on policy and the most recent Ofsted judgment of their school. This may point to school quality and the effectiveness of leaders themselves (Sammons et al., 2006) as an influence on views on policy. Conversely, it may (also) point to the pressures of school performance and accountability in shaping school responses to policy (Ball et al., 2012). The data from the 2012 survey suggest a third dimension is significant. Across a range of policies, government has purposefully differentiated schools by Ofsted judgments (and student attainment). On this basis schools have gained differential access to academy and Teaching School status and different inspection and audit cycles. For some school leaders, this implies easier access to 'autonomy around the edges' of criteria power that Simkins (1997) identified. Headteachers in Class 1 (confident), for instance, anticipated greater autonomy in practice including through TSAs or school chains across which they could influence the character of a school alliance. For other schools, however, 'autonomy around the edges' appeared less accessible as government regulates differently the freedoms schools have to act.

The implications of reform

These perspectives on differentiation between school leader respondents point, finally, to two wider implications of the current reform agenda. The first concerns a hierarchical segmentation among schools. Brian Lightman (2011), the general secretary of the Association of Schools and College Leaders, has talked of 'confident' and 'constrained' schools. Confident schools, he argues, with a 'good' or 'outstanding' Ofsted report and student attainment above the national average, can choose to disregard aspects of policy and develop a long-term vision of leadership and learning. Conversely, constrained schools, close to government floor targets and at risk of an Ofsted visit, are reactive to policy and unable to relax about accountability.

The data from the 2012 landscape study partly bear out this differentiation, but also suggest it misses out a majority of schools that are neither strongly 'confident' nor strongly 'constrained'. Further statistical analysis situated two-thirds of respondents in Classes 2 and 3. These schools have been defined, in the language of Lightman, as *'cautious'* and *'concerned'*. While a simplified typology, summarized as confident, cautious, concerned and constrained (or possibly cynical), the analysis points to how a combination of increasing operational power, declining support from LAs and differential regulation of schools has the potential to intensify local hierarchies that exist between many schools (Waslander et al., 2010).

These potential fault lines point, second, to the importance of external support. With the anticipated decline of many LA functions, government argues schools will gain support from a mixed economy. This will consist of on the one hand, Teaching Schools, academy chains, national leaders of education (NLEs) and other aspects of the so-called self-improving system, and on the other, schools, LAs and commercial organizations selling services within a school improvement market. The data reflected these changes, with schools anticipating a greater diversity of support but also movement away from known and well-used sources. A concern for school leaders focused on replacing an old system, in which the quality of support varied by LA postcodes, with a new system where variations will stem from a complex amalgam, including: the moral purpose of 'confident' schools; the capacity and willingness of schools most in need of support to engage in collaboration and procurement; the motives of for-profit providers; the differing evolutions of LAs. While some school leaders welcomed access to a wider pool of services, for most it was unclear whether this patchwork of provision would provide appropriate and equitable support.

Conclusion

This chapter has drawn upon the 2012 landscape study to consider school leaders' views on school autonomy, as it exists within the wider educational policy framework. School leaders commonly anticipated greater power over aspects of school management but not over the aims and purposes of schooling. Considerable variation was also found in school leaders' perspectives on their freedom and capacity to act. This related to number of factors but most importantly to school phase, size and inspection judgment. On capacity, among smaller and many primary schools there was considerable concern that additional managerial powers and duties would both disrupt a leadership focus on learning and come hand-in-hand with a lack of support. On freedom to act, government was seen to retain tight control over schools, but also to be differentiating control by inspection judgements and national test results. Summarizing the resulting differentiated autonomy for schools, a typology was proposed of *confident, cautious, concerned* and *constrained* schools. A key implication is that increasing operational power for schools, changing external support and differentiated school autonomy have the potential to intensify existing local hierarchies between schools. Headteachers and chairs of governors' views on the policy landscape are considered further in Chapter 5.

3

The Demography of School Leadership

Rebecca Allen and Shenila Rawal

This chapter considers the demographic characteristics of those who are leading schools in England in 2012 and how the state of school leadership has changed over time, particularly in this era of changing school governance and greater autonomy for leadership teams. Understanding the age, sex, ethnicity and subject background profiles of senior leaders in schools is clearly important from a planning perspective, but this is just one reason why understanding who becomes a school leader is important.

As highlighted in the first chapter, school leadership has been suggested to be second only to classroom teaching as an influence on student learning (Day et al., 2009). Even where evidence is mixed on the direct relationship between school leaders and pupil outcomes, the indirect impact that headteachers can have is less contentious and has been the subject of much research (Bruggencate et al., 2012). As explored in more detail in Chapter 7, this indirect impact stems from leaders' influence for example on staff motivation, teaching practices and working conditions. Headteachers' educational values, strategic intelligence and leadership strategies all have a direct impact on school and classroom processes and practices that can in turn result in improvements in pupil outcomes (Day et al., 2009). While the most effective school leaders do not have a particular age, gender or ethnic profile, it is noted that the opportunity to become a school leader varies by these dimensions. This therefore suggests that newly recruited leaders are not being selected from the widest possible pool of applicants which would indicate that the overall effectiveness of school leadership could be improved.

Throughout this chapter the School Workforce Census (SWC) for November 2011 is used to analyse the structure of leadership teams and demographic characteristics of teachers across different types of state-funded schools in England. The job transitions of teachers within and across schools between November 2010 and November 2011 are also examined. The SWC is statutory return of information on all staff from local authorities, state-maintained schools and academies in England and was first taken in November 2010. Unfortunately comparable data are not available for earlier periods of this study so the chapter's focus is predominantly the period covered by the SWC. The SWC contains a basic record for every individual working in a school. In this chapter the particular focus is on senior leadership, that is, headteachers, deputy heads and assistant heads. The age, sex, and ethnic and subject backgrounds of senior leaders in schools are examined. Also explored are the differences in tenure in their current school, hours spent teaching, promotion rates and choices of school to work in. This analysis of school leadership demography provides a description of the state of the current teacher labour market, relative to past trends wherever possible.

The teacher labour market and school leadership teams

The SWC shows the numbers of teachers within each post for 2010 and 2011. At this time there were approximately half a million teachers in post in just over 21,000 state schools. In the majority of cases the posts remain the same across the two years. Secondary school senior leadership teams (SLTs) tend to reflect a classic management hierarchy or pyramid, with more deputies than headteachers and more assistant heads than deputies. By contrast, primary school leadership structures are reversed because many small primaries have no senior leadership roles below that of headteacher (Table 3.1).

From the November 2011 SWC data, 410 executive headteachers can be identified, which is less than an estimate of 450 executive heads based on a sample of data (National College, 2010). Where a school has an executive head, in the vast majority of cases (99%) they are clearly also the substantive headteacher. According to guidance from the Department for Education (DfE), schools should only use this classification if the headteacher in question directly leads two or more schools in a federation or other partnership arrangement.

TABLE 3.1 Size of leadership teams by phase of schooling

	Number of schools with an SLT size of			
	0	1 or 2	3 or 4	5 or more
Secondary schools (n = 3,129)				
Number of headteachers	129	2,982	14	4
Number of deputy heads	323	2,326	421	59
Number of assistant heads	252	826	1,161	890
Primary schools (n = 16,571)				
Number of headteachers	833	16,132	9	0
Number of deputy heads	5,895	11,036	42	1
Number of assistant heads	11,980	4,641	325	28
Special schools (n = 942)				
Number of headteachers	57	887	1	0
Number of deputy heads	181	747	17	0
Number of assistant heads	359	495	83	8

It is therefore possible that the SWC is failing to count executive heads who are not directly employed by a school or Local Authority (LA).

There is relatively little variation in the average structure of leadership teams by school governance type. However, academies tend to have larger leadership teams overall and that voluntary-controlled schools tend to have the smallest leadership teams. In the latter's case this is because they include many small rural primary schools.

Age profile of school leaders

The age profile of school leaders, relative to others in the teacher workforce, is now described along with the implications for future supply in the labour market. Studying the age of teachers is particularly interesting in the absence of a measure of years of teaching experience. The average age of headteachers at November 2011 was 50 years old (51 years for executive headteachers). Assistant and deputy headteacher average ages were 44 and 45 years respectively. The average age of classroom teachers was 39 years; those who appear for the first time in the 2011 SWC are younger at 35 years; and those who are paid at the lowest point on the pay scale are younger still at 34 years. Figure 3.1 shows the age profile for teachers by leadership grouping, separately for secondary and primary schools, with a clear bimodal distribution for most categories of teacher. The upper peak for all groups of teachers is in the late 50s, reflecting the final tail of the demographic bubble in teaching from those born in the first decade after the end of the Second World War.

After their mid-50s it is clear that large numbers take retirement from teaching, often before the official retirement age of 60. Just under a third of all headteachers are aged 55 years and over and the age distribution indicates that almost half of those headteachers who reach the age of 55 then go on to take early retirement somewhere between the ages of 55 and 59 years. This feature of early retirement has been noted in many National Association of Head Teachers (NAHT) leadership reports (Howson, 2010, 2011). These reports suggest that early retirement levels seem to relate to factors such as salary levels and the challenges associated with the job in different types of school. Retirements at age 60 or older have represented a higher percentage than earlier. During the 1990s, premature and early retirement rates were on the increase and peaked in 1997 when the rules governing early retirement changed. For a period after 1997, rates of early retirement were low before increasing again during the early part of the century.

The age of the lower peak varies across leadership levels. For classroom teachers the peak is at age 31, after which some gain promotion into senior leadership and large numbers of female teachers take time out of the labour market to have children. For assistant and deputy head posts, the lower modal ages are 39 and 40 years respectively, reflecting a large number of appointments into these posts during a teacher's 30s and large numbers of first promotions to headship from the late 30s onwards. A relatively large group of assistant and deputy heads who are in their 50s and so unlikely to achieve headship can be observed in both sectors. This is consistent with aspirations data published in 2009 (ICM, 2009) that reported one-third of deputy and assistant heads hoped to progress to headship in the next three years and another third had no plans to become heads.

Figure 3.1 shows that the age profiles differ slightly across schooling phase, with primary school teachers reaching promotion to all leadership levels earlier in their career. This is confirmed in the summary statistics in Table 3.2 and reflects the shorter career trajectory necessary to lead a smaller primary school, compared to a larger secondary school.

It might be expected to see slightly older headteachers leading the larger schools within each phase of education since these larger schools should

TABLE 3.2 Average age profile of teachers (in years)

	Secondary schools	Primary schools	Special schools
	mean	mean	mean
Headteacher	51.0	49.1	51.8
Deputy headteacher	47.0	43.2	49.1
Assistant headteacher	44.7	42.5	47.2
Classroom teacher	38.8	38.4	43.3

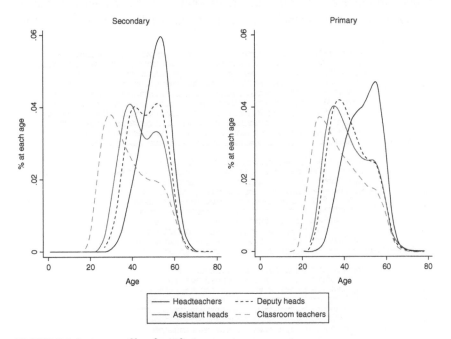

FIGURE 3.1 *Age profile of teachers.*

offer higher salaries to reflect more complex organizations and greater financial resources. Surprisingly though, the difference in mean average age of headteachers between the largest and smallest school is small, although statistically significant, at almost one year for both primary schools and secondary schools. The reverse is true for classroom teachers, who are younger on average in the larger schools.

Figure 3.2 shows the age profile of teachers by region. As expected, classroom teachers and assistant heads in inner London are younger than all other regions, but this trend is not significant for the more senior levels of leadership. This very slight difference between London and other regions is surprisingly small and may reflect the success in retaining teachers within the capital through the increasing generosity of the London-specific pay scales from 2003 onwards. There is also no difference in the average age of headteachers and deputy heads across school governance type or demographic of student intake, although sponsored academies and the most deprived schools have younger assistant heads and classroom teachers.

In secondary schools the average age of first promotions to assistant, deputy and head is 39, 42 and 45 years respectively. Perhaps surprisingly, it is not much different for primary schools: the average age of first promotions to assistant, deputy and heads is 38, 40 and 42 years respectively.

Overall the peak age of promotion to first headship is from the late 30s through to the late 40s. Promotion to headteacher can happen well into an individual's 50s; more so for internal promotions than for external promotions.

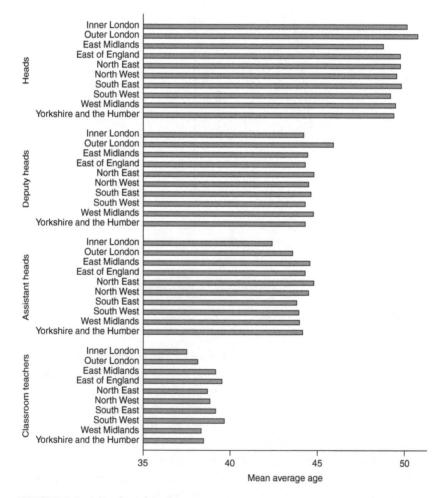

FIGURE 3.2 *Age of teachers by region.*

The fact that internal promotions dominate later in a career suggests these may be temporary appointments in the event of sickness/maternity cover or failure to appoint following advertisement. Where deputy heads choose to take on a second deputy appointment at a new school, this tends to happen relatively early in their career (in an individual's 30s to mid-40s).

For assistant heads, moves to other schools peak at around the age of 35. Promotions to a new school tend to decline quite rapidly from this stage onwards, whereas there is a small peak during the mid-50s for internal promotions that may simply reflect large numbers of teachers who are currently of this age.

Large numbers of classroom teachers leave the profession during their 20s, either permanently or temporarily for family or other reasons. Large numbers of those in their 20s also move to become a classroom teacher at a new school. Promotions to assistant head generally take place during teachers' 30s, with external promotions at new schools happening earlier than internal promotions.

Gender profile of school leaders

Teaching remains a female-dominated profession – more so in the primary than the secondary sector. However, Table 3.3 shows that smaller proportions of women than men move into each stage of senior leadership. The differences are particularly pronounced in the age range 30–39, where 88 and 65 per cent of classroom teachers in this range are female, in the primary and secondary sectors respectively, yet only 60 and 20 per cent of headteachers in this age range are female. The early successful promotion of men within the profession may, in part, reflect women taking a slower career path during childbearing years since by their fifties they have caught up a little with 76 and 41 per cent of headteachers in this age range being female in the primary and secondary sectors respectively.

Clearly the data are limited in the extent to which they can explain why men achieve more successful career progression than women teachers. As well as time taken out of the labour market by women for childrearing, the behaviour of men may differ in other ways. For example, a survey by McNamara et al. (2010) found that men apply for significantly more leadership posts than women before being appointed, feel less constrained by child care choices they have to make and are more prepared to move regionally for a new post than their female counterparts. School Workforce Census data confirm that male senior leaders do achieve promotion through a regional move more frequently than females at the same rank.

For those school leaders who are identifiable in both 2010 and 2011 censuses, Table 3.3 indicates their post-transitions in that one-year period.

TABLE 3.3 Gender profile of teachers

	Age ≤29		Age 30–39		Age 40–49		Age 50–59		Age ≥60	
	N	% female	N	% female	N	% female	N	% female	N	% female
Secondary schools										
Head	0		161	20	1,033	35	1,808	41	206	36
Deputy head	15	53	1,024	41	2,114	41	1,985	50	177	38
Assistant head	170	52	3,600	49	3,952	48	3,573	55	301	54
Classroom teacher	48,817	69	66,578	65	43,950	62	36,419	62	5,818	54
Primary schools										
Head	14	64	2,054	60	6,074	69	7,447	76	919	75
Deputy head	276	79	4,523	75	3,996	79	2,900	86	291	87
Assistant head	360	77	2,994	83	2,176	84	1,832	92	173	88
Classroom teacher	48,961	88	59,486	88	42,270	90	31,426	92	5,049	88

The vast majority of teachers remain at the same school without promotion each year. For those who achieve promotion at each level, females are consistently more likely to achieve it through internal promotion rather than external promotion. It is not known whether this is because female teachers have closer interpersonal relations with their colleagues that increase either their chances of or desire for internal promotion at the same school.

Alternatively, women may be geographically constrained by family commitments so do not feel able to apply to other schools. Similarly, male teachers may seek promotion in new schools if they feel under pressure to move up through the pay scale quickly. Regardless of reasons, this greater propensity of women to wait for an appropriate internal promotion to arise is consistent with McNamara et al.'s (2010) observation that women apply for fewer jobs, and provides a further explanation as to why the careers of female teachers progress more slowly than those of male teachers.

Ethnic background of school leaders

Teaching remains largely a White profession, with 90 per cent of teachers reporting they are of a White ethnic background. These figures do represent a 5 percentage point decrease over official statistics collected between 2003 and 2008, which suggested that 95 per cent of teachers were of White ethnicity (McNamara et al., 2009), although the change may be greater in certain parts of the country. However, teachers are still not representative of the current student population, where around 80 per cent of pupils are of White ethnicity. This divide is particularly wide in some of the urban areas. Over 95 per cent of headteachers report they are of a White ethnic background, which is clearly a higher rate than for teachers as a whole. In part this is not surprising given the age demographic of headteachers. The only other ethnic groups that are represented with over 100 headteachers are those of Indian and of Black Caribbean ethnicity. This apparent lack of minority ethnic groups in school leadership teams confirms that the findings of Ross in 2003 still hold true today.

Ethnic minorities are clearly under-represented in SLTs, both relative to current student demographics and to the ethnic mix of teachers overall. How much this is due to the older age profile of senior leaders and how much is due to ethnic minority groups not gaining promotion, given promotion rates by White British teachers of the same age, is now explored. Formally, this is done by modelling the proportion of teachers who are senior leaders for each age, gender and ethnic group. Regression analysis shows the rates of promotion by ethnicity, age and sex in a chart (Figure 3.3).

Figure 3.3 shows that overall the chances of being a senior leader is lower for all ethnic groups compared to the White British group. For women (dotted lines on the chart), it shows that the proportions who are senior leaders at

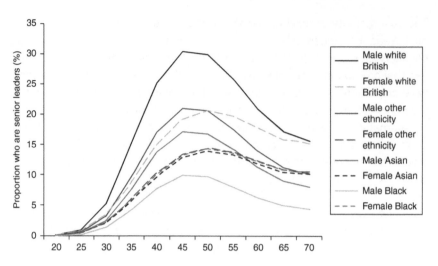

FIGURE 3.3 *Proportions who are senior leaders by age, sex and ethnicity.*

each age group is the same for the White other, Asian and Black groups, but that all of these rates are significantly lower than for White British teachers. For men (solid lines on the chart), the differences across ethnic groups are very pronounced. White British men are by far the most successful at making it to senior leadership, followed by White other ethnicity, then Asian ethnicity. The male Black teachers are by far the most under-represented group within senior leadership roles in schools. Another interpretation is that the male-female promotional gap is much smaller for Asian and Black ethnic groups than it is for White British groups, suggesting a greater relative promotional disadvantage for male ethnic minorities.

Of course, this analysis is simply descriptive and says nothing about why this under-representation of ethnic minority groups occurs. For example, although age and sex are taken into account, any differences in age at entry into teaching or differences in qualification levels of these groups is not taken into account. Furthermore, for some teachers the decision to remain as a classroom teacher rather than move into leadership is a positive choice, and it is possible that this choice varies by ethnic background.

By contrast, those ethnic minority teachers who do make it to a senior leadership position do not significantly differ in their chances of gaining further promotion compared to their White British counterparts with similar characteristics. This contrasts with their lower likelihood of progressing into senior leadership for the first time.

Ethnic minority teachers and senior leaders have some tendency to cluster in schools with larger proportions of ethnic minority students. Figure 3.4 is a pie chart reporting the ethnic profile of school leaders across six different

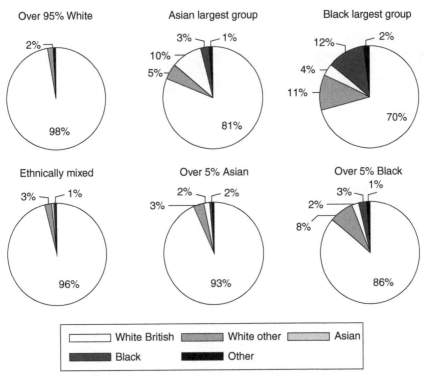

Graphs by ethnic mix of school

FIGURE 3.4 *Ethnic profile of senior leaders by ethnicity of students.*

types of school (e.g. schools where over 95% of the students are of White ethnic origin; schools where Black students form the largest ethnic group; schools where over 5% of pupils are of Asian ethnic background). Although White British teachers continue to dominate in all types of schools, ethnic minority teachers tend to cluster in schools where pupils share their own ethnic background. Ethnic minority teachers are under-represented at senior leadership levels. Figure 3.4 shows that 12 per cent of senior leaders are of Black ethnic origin in schools where Black students form the largest ethnic group and 10 per cent of senior leaders are Asian in schools where Asian students form the largest ethnic group. For headteachers, the equivalent percentages fall again to 11 per cent and 8 per cent respectively.

Pay of senior leaders

Teacher pay has become increasingly deregulated as the number of academies who can deviate from national pay and conditions increases. There has been a long period of relative flexibility on the part of governing bodies as to how

TABLE 3.4 Distribution of pay of senior leaders by school phase – 2011

	N	5th percentile	25th percentile	50th percentile	75th percentile	95th percentile
Secondary schools						
Heads	3,211	£54,342	£76,409	£86,365	£95,587	£112,000
Deputy Heads	5,314	£46,690	£58,362	£62,811	£67,602	£76,409
Assistant Heads	11,596	£42,320	£49,130	£52,900	£55,553	£62,784
Classroom Teachers	201,635	£13,977	£25,168	£34,181	£40,433	£47,458
Primary schools						
Heads	16,502	£42,379	£51,398	£55,834	£62,640	£74,686
Deputy Heads	11,988	£32,599	£42,379	£45,637	£49,130	£57,985
Assistant Heads	7,491	£27,382	£40,339	£42,379	£45,637	£52,900
Classroom Teachers	187,188	£10,233	£21,588	£29,105	£35,447	£40,981
Special schools						
Heads	925	£50,359	£62,811	£69,275	£78,003	£92,938
Deputy Heads	930	£43,521	£50,359	£54,305	£59,809	£68,375
Assistant Heads	1,092	£35,620	£45,337	£48,024	£51,302	£57,445
Classroom Teachers	13,689	£13,283	£25,296	£34,166	£39,983	£45,405

Note: Maximum and minimum pay are not reported due to concerns over data accuracy at these extremes.

much to pay their headteacher. Table 3.4 shows the pay distribution of teachers by post and phase of schooling in 2011. Pay at secondary schools is more generous than at primary schools for every level of responsibility. This is logical given that primary school teachers have less experience at time of promotion and also run smaller and less complex organizations. The variation in the pay of headteachers at secondary schools is striking, compared to relatively little variation in pay for deputy and assistant heads.

Academies pay their headteachers more (over £2,500) than other types of schools, even when school characteristics, pay region, social and ethnic mix of school, age, sex and ethnicity of teacher are taken into account. This relative generosity in pay does not trickle down to less senior teachers: Academies appear to pay their deputies and assistants just over £2,000 less than other schools when accounting for the age and sex of the teachers in their school. This analysis of Academy pay is consistent with that of the DfE (2011) who report that the lower pay of classroom teachers is entirely due to their younger age mix.

Overall there is little difference in pay for classroom teachers by school characteristics suggesting that most other schools are sticking to the nationally agreed pay scales. However, governing bodies appear to use flexibilities to pay headteachers and deputy/assistants more where recruitment is difficult, for example in schools with more deprived pupil intakes. Larger schools also pay all their teachers higher salaries, which might simply reflect greater flexibility in their budgets.

Older deputy/assistant head and classroom teachers are paid more, however there is no such age-related difference for headteachers. Female teachers are paid less than male teachers across all levels of leadership. Older teachers are paid more at lower levels of leadership. Both these associations simply reflect years of teaching experience. Asian minority headteachers are paid a little more than equivalent headteachers of other ethnicities. There is no such significant difference in relation to assistant/deputy headteachers. As regards classroom teachers, all ethnic minorities display lower levels of pay than White classroom teachers. It is not clear why this might be the case and may reflect differences in age at entry into the profession for these groups or fewer accumulated responsibility points.

Tenure of senior leaders

This section explores the tenure profile of senior leaders across schools, as measured by total numbers of years in their current school and total number of years under their current contract. Figure 3.5 reports these statistics across type of school and leadership post. Clearly, the average years under current contract is lower than the average years in school and differences between the two could indicate internal promotions. However, the number of teachers at each level that appear to be in their first year of contract is a little high, given the known job vacancy rates across the sector and so this variable has not been used for the remainder of this section. A 2011 NAHT survey (Howson, 2011) recorded 22 per cent internal appointments for permanent head vacancies in the primary sector, compared to the one-third implied in SWC; it is possible that the differences are explained by temporary and acting appointments.

Figure 3.5 shows relatively long tenures for secondary school deputy and assistant heads, which is suggestive of the extent of internal promotion into these positions. By contrast, average tenure for headteachers is significantly shorter. Tenure is shorter for all senior positions within primary schools, perhaps because their smaller size means that appropriate promotion opportunities arise less frequently within the school. The issue of 'post blocking' and its implications for promotional opportunities and the size of the potential headship pool have been discussed elsewhere (Howson, 2010).

Figure 3.6 shows the tenure distribution, measured as total time in school, for different levels of current post. Rather surprisingly, the tenure distributions are very similar across senior leadership and classroom teaching posts, although average tenure is shorter for classroom teachers. Over 13 per cent of teachers – about one-in-eight – have been in their current school for less than a year. About a quarter of teachers have taught in their current school for over ten years and 1.5 per cent for over 30 years.

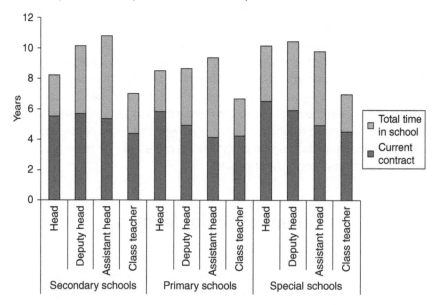

FIGURE 3.5 *Average tenure in school versus current contract.*

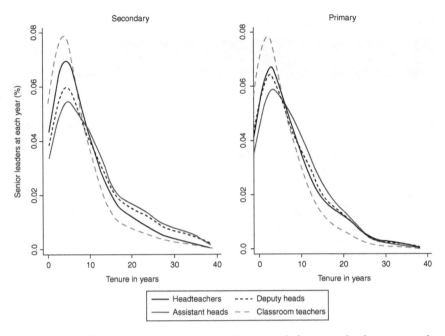

FIGURE 3.6 *Tenure (years in school since first arrival) for senior leaders in second-ary and primary schools.*

Further analysis explored how tenure varies by characteristics of school and teacher, separately for posts in primary and secondary schools (see Table 3.5). In the secondary sector, there is some evidence that tenure for headteachers at foundation and voluntary-aided schools may be slightly longer than the mean. Regional differences in tenure length are very slight for headteachers and longest for classroom teachers. In general, tenure is longer in the north of England and shortest in the south-east and London. Teachers in large schools have slightly longer tenure, which may reflect greater internal promotion opportunities. Schools with deprived student intakes have shorter tenure for all teachers. This association between deprivation in school and headteacher tenure is consistent with earlier studies (e.g. Chapman and Harris, 2004).

In primary schools, regional patterns of tenure length are visible across all leadership levels, with short tenure in the South East, London and East Midlands regions, and longer tenure in the North West and North East regions. Primary schools with a disadvantaged pupil intake have shorter tenure for all teacher posts. Larger schools have slightly longer tenure for classroom teachers. Female headteachers have shorter tenure than male headteachers in primary schools, which may reflect a later age of first appointment. However, they have longer tenure at the deputy and assistant head, and classroom teacher

TABLE 3.5 Modelling variation in tenure (i.e. total time in school)

	Headteachers		Deputy and assistants	Classroom teachers
Secondary schools				
School governance	Voluntary-aided and foundation schools have longer tenure	Academies have shorter tenure	Academies have shorter tenure	Academies have shorter tenure
Regions	East Midlands, East of England and South East regions have shortest		Shortest in South East region	Short in outer London, East Midlands, East of England and South East regions; longest in North West and North East regions
Grammar schools	No difference		No difference	Tenure longer
Urbanness and deprivation level	More deprived schools have shorter tenure		More deprived schools have shorter tenure	More deprived schools have shorter tenure
Number of students	Larger schools slightly longer		Larger schools slightly longer	Larger schools slightly longer
Age of teacher	Little difference		Older teachers have longer tenure	Older teachers have longer tenure
Sex of teacher	No difference		Female teachers have shorter tenure	Female teachers have shorter tenure
Ethnicity of teacher	No difference		Black and other minorities have shorter tenure	All ethnic minorities have shorter tenure

	Headteachers	Deputy and assistants	Classroom teachers
		Primary schools	
School governance	No differences	Academies have shorter tenure; foundation schools have longer	Academies have shorter tenure
Regions	Shorter in outer London, East Midlands, East of England, South East, South West and West Midlands regions	Shorter in outer London, East Midlands and South East regions	Longest in North West and North East regions
Urban-rural, deprivation	More deprived schools have slightly shorter tenure	More deprived schools have slightly shorter tenure	More deprived schools have slightly shorter tenure
Number of pupils	Little difference	Little difference	Larger schools slightly longer
Age of teacher	Little difference	Older teachers have longer tenure	Older teachers have longer tenure
Sex of teacher	Female teachers have shorter tenure	Female teachers have slightly longer tenure	Female teachers have slightly longer tenure
Ethnicity of teacher	No difference	Black and other minorities have shorter tenure	All minorities have shorter tenure

level. This is consistent with McNamara et al. (2010) who report that male teachers move school more frequently before achieving a leadership role. Finally, there is some evidence that those of Black and other ethnic minority background have shorter tenure in general at the primary school level.

Overall promotion rates

As shown earlier in this chapter, females generally are less likely than males to achieve a promotion (holding constant their other characteristics) and that the chances of promotion peaks in a deputy's 40s and a classroom teacher's 20s (the promotion window for the assistant head is dispersed across a very large age range).

How promotion takes place is now examined by looking at the chances of achieving promotion at a new school rather than at the same school. Female teachers are much less likely to seek external promotion rather than internal promotion at all levels of senior leadership. External promotion also becomes relatively infrequent for promotions of classroom teachers over 50 years of age. There are no ethnic differences in the use of internal versus external promotion, once other teacher characteristics are taken into account. For all levels of promotion, the longer a teacher has been in their current school, the more likely they are to seek and achieve an internal promotion.

Segmentation of the teacher labour market

How segmented the teacher labour market appears to be, both regionally and by school governance types, can be analysed by seeing how frequently new teacher appointments involve a move across region or governance type. Generally the regions of London, the East of England and the East Midlands make the most appointments from a different region. Across the country, geographical moves are generally more prevalent for sideways moves than they are for promotions and are far more prevalent at more junior ranks than for the most senior roles. This suggests that non-career motives dominate long-distance job moves and also suggests that senior teachers become increasingly constrained by family commitments in their choice of school.

Table 3.6 explores whether new appointments tend to be made to teachers who have come from a school of the same type of governance. This segmentation of the teacher labour market appears to happen even for sideways moves of classroom teachers. This is consistently true across all sectors, but is most pronounced for voluntary-aided schools, where 37 per cent of all new appointments to classroom teacher roles (excluding newly qualified teacher [NQT] appointments) are made to teachers who have previously taught in voluntary-aided schools. If these appointments were made at random, the figure would be just 16 per cent. What is interesting is how pronounced this segmentation becomes for all senior leadership roles in all sectors. Once again, in the voluntary-aided sector, the proportion of

TABLE 3.6 Sector origin for new appointments (external and internal) by school governance

2011	Headteachers	Deputy headteachers	Assistant headteachers	Classroom teachers
From another sector				
Academy	13	40	106	1,347
Community	249	196	146	3,145
Foundation	61	53	106	1,921
Voluntary aided	120	80	68	1,780
Voluntary controlled	162	74	35	931
From same sector				
Academy	19	67	128	135
Community	1,039	1,490	1,856	6,503
Foundation	92	179	427	924
Voluntary aided	340	428	474	1,039
Voluntary controlled	155	152	156	198

appointments made to teachers currently in the same sector is 74 per cent, 84 per cent and 87 per cent for headteachers, deputy heads and assistant heads respectively.

These figures are equally high for Roman Catholic (RC) schools, with recruitment of teachers from other RC schools standing at 88 per cent, 90 per cent, 90 per cent and 45 per cent for heads, deputies, assistant heads and classroom teachers respectively. This desire to recruit within sector clearly restricts choice of appointment and so may explain the appointment difficulties experienced within this sector.

Of course it is not possible to explain why this stark segmentation is taking place; in particular, whether this represents the choices of teachers in job application patterns or whether it is more due to the preferences of the schools for particular teachers. In addition, it is important to bear in mind that some of the segmentation is due to the geographical clustering of particular school governance types and internal promotions that will be taking place.

Subject background of senior leaders

The SWC provides information on the academic subject that teachers took their most advanced qualification in. However, there is a lot of missing data and the Bachelor of Education degree, which many primary teachers possess, is not subject specific. The data suggest that in secondary schools, those with a background in humanities are most likely to progress through to headteacher (this is also somewhat true for English in SWC but not in other datasets). Interestingly, for historical comparison, a study of the cohort of all secondary heads appointed to their first posts in England and Wales in 1982–83 found humanities (38%) and English (24%) to be their main subject backgrounds (Weindling and Earley, 1987). In the SWC data, those with a background in maths, languages and sciences do progress to assistant and deputy head positions, but the proportions who make it to headteacher are significantly lower. In primary and special schools, very few teachers have subject qualifications in maths, languages or sciences, although those who have a maths or science qualification do successfully progress to leadership positions.

Changes in the leadership landscape

In this final section of the chapter, changes in the leadership landscape and prospects for changes in the future, particularly in the light of constrained school budgets, are reflected upon. Much of the data in this section is not taken from the SWC and in the case of Vactrak, not from government data.

Table 3.7 shows changes in the number of senior leaders and other staff from 2005 onwards (taken from Table 1 in a Department for Education statistical first release (SFR) dated April 2012). According to these data, the number of teachers and senior leaders peaked in 2010 and has started falling, but only a little. Looking further back into the past, the large rise in the number of teaching assistants over this period has resulted in each headteacher managing a larger staff, on average. However, other data show that the rise in the number of assistant heads means that the number of employees at a school per senior leadership team (SLT) member is unchanged.

Table 3.8 shows the age distribution of headteachers in 2000 and 2010. There are now more teachers achieving headship in their 30s, but also considerably more heads in their late 50s and 60s. Caution is needed in interpreting the table however due to the large percentage of 'not known' for primary heads in 2000. Retirement pressure does seem containable overall.

TABLE 3.7 Changes in the number of senior leaders and school staff between 2005 and 2011 (thousands)

	January						November	
	2005	2006	2007	2008	2009	2010	2010	2011
Full-time headteachers	21.5	21.3	21.1	20.6	20.4	20.0	20.5	20.1
Full-time deputy heads	18.8	18.2	18.0	17.4	17.3	17.0	17.5	17.3
Full-time assistant heads	12.5	13.8	16.2	17.4	17.9	17.9	18.8	19.2
Part-time FTE leadership	1.0	1.4	1.8	2.2	2.8	3.6	.	3.4
Total FTE qualified teachers	415.4	420.2	422.1	423.6	425.2	432	430.3	422.2
Total FTE unqualified teachers	18.8	18.2	17.2	17.5	17.4	16	17.8	15.8
Head count occasional teachers	–	–	–	–	–	–	12.2	11.5
Total teachers	–	–	–	–	–	–	460.3	449.5
Teaching assistants	96.6	103.1	112.3	126.1	132.4	143.3	–	194
Special needs support	48.1	47.7	48.5	47.9	48.4	48.1	–	24.9
Minority ethnic support	2.6	2.7	3	3	2.9	2.9	–	0.9
Total teaching assistants	147.2	153.5	163.8	177	183.7	194.2	213.9	219.8
Administrative staff	59	63	66.7	69.7	73.1	75.6	–	79.9
Other support staff	59.6	72.6	77.7	79.9	89.1	93	–	179.3
Total FTE workforce	700.1	727.6	747.5	767.7	788.5	810.9	850.1	875.9

Source: DfE SFR using Form 618g (teachers) and the school census (support staff) (January 2002, 2010) and School Workforce Census (November 2010 and 2011).

TABLE 3.8 Age distribution of headteachers in 2000 and 2010 (% share of total)

	<30 yrs %	30–34 yrs %	35–39 yrs %	40–44 yrs %	45–49 yrs %	50–54 yrs %	55–59 yrs %	60+ yrs%	Not known%
Primary schools									
Mar 2000	0.1	1.7	5.4	13.4	30.4	22.1	13.4	1.9	11.4
Nov 2010	0.1	2.1	10.5	16.1	19.0	22.7	24.4	5.1	0.0
Secondary schools									
Mar 2000	0.0	0.0	1.9	12.2	30.7	36.6	17.3	2.8	1.4
Nov 2010	0.0	0.4	4.4	10.4	20.7	30.5	27.6	6.0	0.0
Special schools									
Mar 2000	0.0	0.7	4.6	15.5	32.0	31.7	14.5	1.2	0.1
Nov 2010	0.0	1.1	3.5	8.5	16.5	32.4	32.9	5.2	0.0

Source: Department for Education and Employment (2000) *Statistics of Education: Teachers England and Wales 2000 Edition.* London: The Stationery Office; and *School Workforce Census* (November 2010).

About 1,500 headteachers retire and/or retire early each year (about 7% of schools).

Looking to the future, job advertisement rates give an indication of changes in demand for senior leadership jobs. In theory, job advertisement rates should mirror the total number of resignations or retirements, less any posts that governors decide not to retain. One obvious response to more constrained budgets is to reduce the number of senior leadership positions. The data suggest that a contraction in the number of deputy and assistant headteacher positions may have started as early as 2009, but that the rate of contraction has speeded up considerably.

This fall in new appointments reduces the size of the pool of candidates for promotion from these grades. Thus, with around 2,500 headships advertised annually, the loss of 700 deputy head and a similar number of assistant head

TABLE 3.9 Teacher vacancies from 2000 onwards

	Vacancies as a percentage of teachers in post								
	2000	2005	2006	2007	2008	2009	Jan 2010	Nov 2010	Nov 2011
Nursery and primary school									
Headteacher	0.8	0.7	0.7	0.6	0.6	0.6	0.7	0.1	0.1
Deputy/assistant head	1.3	0.8	0.9	0.7	1.0	1.0	0.5	0.3	0.3
Classroom teacher	0.8	0.4	0.3	0.3	0.4	0.4	0.3	0.1	0.1
Secondary school (maintained only)									
Headteacher	1.1	1.0	0.9	0.5	0.6	0.7	0.7	0.1	0.0
Deputy/assistant head	0.9	0.5	0.5	0.4	0.4	0.3	0.3	0.1	0.2
Classroom teacher	0.7	0.9	0.7	0.7	0.8	0.8	0.5	0.1	0.1
Special school									
Headteacher	2.5	0.9	1.6	1.2	0.7	1.1	0.8	0.1	0.2
Deputy/assistant head	2.6	1.5	1.4	1.4	1.1	1.4	0.8	0.2	0.2
Classroom teacher	1.8	1.7	1.6	1.4	1.5	1.4	0.9	0.1	0.2
Academy									
Headteacher								0.0	0.0
Deputy/assistant head								0.5	0.2
Classroom teacher								0.2	0.1

Source: Department for Education (2012) *School Workforce in England November 2011*, Statistical First Release SFR06/2012 (25 April 2012).

vacancies will have an impact in the future on the pool of candidates applying for promotion.

The data on teacher vacancies over time in Table 3.9 mirrors the advertisement data that suggest a large fall in demand for deputy and assistant heads, particularly in primary schools. The vacancy rates in the November 2010 SWC look very low across the board, but this undoubtedly reflects the timing of the data collection early in the school year. The figures for November 2011 are little different.

Conclusion

In this chapter the SWC for November 2010 and November 2011 (DfE, 2010a, 2011) have been used to analyse the structure of leadership teams and demographic characteristics of school leaders and teachers across different types of state-funded schools in England. In particular, the job transitions of school teachers and leaders, their age, sex, ethnic and subject background, differences in pay and tenure, promotion rates and choices of school were presented. Some key findings emerge:

- Just under a third of all headteachers are aged 55 years and over. Almost half of those headteachers who reach the age of 55 then go on to take early retirement somewhere between the ages of 55 and 59 years.

- There are more teachers achieving headship in their 30s, but also considerably more heads in their late 50s and 60s.

- The average age of first promotions to assistant, deputy and head was 39, 41 and 43 years respectively (the phase difference was small).

- Over 90 per cent of schools still follow a standard model of one headteacher (i.e. not shared and not executive).

- The typical structure for leadership teams in primary schools remains one head and one deputy.

- Secondaries are more variable but typically have one head, one or two deputies and three or four assistants.

- Academies have larger SLTs with more deputies and assistant heads.

- Teachers with a background in humanities are most likely to progress through to secondary headship.

- In primary and special schools, very few teachers have a maths or science qualification, although those that do often successfully progress to leadership positions.

The analysis of the quantitative data on school leadership demography and the labour market highlights four key observations.

First, although teaching clearly continues to be a female-dominated profession, it is striking the extent to which smaller proportions of women than men moved into each stage of senior leadership. The differences were particularly pronounced in the age range 30–39, where 88 per cent of primary classroom teachers and 64 per cent of secondary classroom teachers in this range were female, yet only 60 per cent of primary and 20 per cent of secondary headteachers in this age range were female. The census data shows that male teachers were more likely to make long-distance geographical job moves in order to achieve promotion, while female teachers choose to make far greater use of internal promotions at their existing school.

Secondly, the teacher labour market was segmented with relatively little movement between geographic regions or even between school governance types. Voluntary-aided schools displayed the highest likelihood of employing teachers who have previously worked within their sector. Senior leadership posts were far more segmented both regionally and by governance type than classroom teacher posts, and senior leaders became increasingly constrained geographically by family and other considerations, compared with the relatively younger pool of classroom teachers. The data suggest that particular types of school have very strong preferences for senior leaders who share a religion, and previous work experience in schools with a similar ethos.

Third, the issue of deputy head turnover was important. The data suggest a reduction of such posts and little turnover and thus a degree of 'blocking' promotional opportunities. Turnover of such posts is important to ensure a pool of applicants for headship going forward to prevent possible future shortages, particularly important during a period of succession planning challenges and changes to the policy landscape. Currently about 1,500 heads retire each year (about 7% of schools).

Finally, teacher pay has become increasingly deregulated with growing numbers of academies that can deviate from national pay scales. Secondary school teacher pay is higher than that at primary schools and the pay of headteachers displays more variation than that of deputy and assistant heads. Academies tend to pay their headteachers more generously than other school types but this is not the case for less senior teachers. In most instances, where pay differences emerge these tend to be due to differences in the level of experience of those teachers.

The availability of two SWC has enabled the linking of teachers across years to study transitions between posts. It has proved possible to study the characteristics of teachers who achieve promotion and levels of segmentation in the teacher labour market. In order to develop a greater understanding of these findings, the following is proposed:

- First, although very significant differences in patterns of promotion between male and female teachers are observed, the data cannot explain fully why they occur and also cannot suggest policy interventions to help female teachers, should they be required. It would be particularly interesting to investigate spatial distances in job moves in more detail within SWC, and also to use survey work to ask what types of constraint female teachers feel they face and why they make such high use of internal promotions.

- Second, the findings related to the continued under-representation of ethnic minority teachers in SLTs suggest that under-representation will not be corrected by simply waiting for young, ethnic minority teachers to reach an age where promotion to higher positions typically takes place. The analysis cannot explain why this is happening, but the SWC does allow lower cost survey work to be conducted because it names the schools taught in for all ethnic minority teachers.

- Third, segmentation of the teacher labour market by school governance is particularly interesting and there are several reasons why it might be occurring. In order to understand it further, the whole process of job advertisement, from applications and interviews through to appointments, needs to be studied.

- Fourth, the issue of acting head and deputy head turnover is important. The data suggest a reduction of such posts and a degree of 'blocking' or limited promotional opportunities. Turnover of such posts ensures a pool of applicants for headship going forward to prevent possible future shortages.

- Finally, there will always be a significant number of heads reaching retirement age each year (approximately 1,500 at the time of the SWCs) because that post is usually a person's last appointment. However, after a period of above-average number of retirements there may be a greater proportion of younger heads in post than previously. Some turnover during the next few years will result from some of these heads changing schools. Turnover may also be affected by the range of other posts available to heads, including any further development of the executive head grade. However, the age profile of headteachers is higher than it was in 2000 and the issue of retirement remains a challenge for the sector.

4

Current Models of Leadership and Future Challenges

This chapter consider two aspects of the changing leadership landscape. It begins by describing models of leadership and school organization and how these have changed over the years. In 2012 the vast majority of headteachers reported being the sole headteacher of a single school working with a single governing body although examples were found of executive headship and collaborative governance arrangements as part of a federation or an academy chain. The size and membership of senior leadership teams (SLTs) are also discussed. These different models and organizational arrangements and how they have changed over time are discussed with reference to future trends and developments as we move towards a self-improving system. Leadership approaches, recruitment and retention and the levels of involvement in leadership tasks and activities by various members of the school community are also discussed with governors' leadership role being the focus of the next chapter.

The second part of this chapter considers the most significant challenges faced by school leaders and compares these challenges with those mentioned in earlier studies. The main concern for school leaders in the 2012 study, for example, was financial, with four out of ten headteachers, one-third of governors and a quarter of senior/middle leaders anticipating finance/budget issues and reductions in funding/austerity measures as one of the key challenges faced. The importance of raising standards was also noted as it was in previous studies.

Models of organization and leadership

Data on models of leadership and school organization were not collected by the first two leadership baseline studies in 2002 and 2005 which tended to concentrate more on the attributes and characteristics of individual school leaders rather than the structural configurations of the organizations in which they worked. The ten school case studies reported in the first baseline study (Earley et al., 2002) provide some background information about organizational structures and notes how all the schools had developed strong and effective senior teams. The 2005 study did not conduct case studies or collect survey data about headship models or organizational structures. However, the 2007 study did and made reference to five different models and it is to these that attention is now given before considering the main findings about leadership models from the 2012 landscape study.

Models of school leadership in the mid-2000s

The 2007 report notes that the ways in which school leadership was structured in the mid-2000s were evolving and claimed from their research that it was evident that:

> there is a high level of diversity in school models, not just in the way in which schools are organized internally but also in their partnerships with external organizations. Much of this diversity is driven by the specific contexts in which schools are operating. (PwC, 2007, p. 48)

They refer to five 'high level leadership models':

- Traditional
- Managed
- Multi-agency managed
- Federated
- System leadership

These models, it is claimed, are necessarily broad and are not mutually exclusive: 'some schools may sit across the boundaries of each category such as those which are providing extended services through multi-agency working and sharing these across a federation of schools' (PwC, p. 49). The 2007 report notes that despite this, 'these models have been recognised and validated by many of the stakeholders consulted throughout the research' (p. 49). Each has potential benefits but if they are to be effective, 'learning-centred leadership should remain firmly at the heart of all models' (p. 49) (this form of leadership is discussed in the next chapter).

The 2007 report argued that these five models of school leadership increasingly characterized the system in the mid-2000s. In part this was in response to workload pressures but also to wider government policies at the time, including the every child matters (ECM) agenda. While effective leadership practices were required across all five models, leaders had to respond flexibly to the context in which they worked which underlined the need 'for the strategic perspective and an ability to "scan the horizon" in order to anticipate future challenges' (p. 51). The 2007 report also notes that:

> effective models are those in which leadership is distributed appropriately at all levels of the organization, there are clear channels of communication, and staff feel that their role and opinions are valued and respected. (p. 51)

The first model is the *traditional* one, with the SLT comprised exclusively of qualified teachers including a headteacher, one or two deputies and/or several assistant heads. Although this model was found across all school types and phases it was more common in the primary sector, especially in small schools. In the PricewaterhouseCoopers (PwC) survey which took place in late 2006, 71 per cent of heads reported that they had no senior support staff on the SLT. Four-fifths (79%) of primaries had no senior support staff compared to 40 per cent of secondaries and 41 per cent of special schools. This model was reflected in the comments of several respondents who thought that, 'in the main, there had been few changes to models in schools despite the changing educational landscape' (p. 54). For example, as a stakeholder respondent commented 'the models of school leadership by and large remain traditional models of school leadership and that puts the pressure on in that the heads have simply embraced more things in the role' (p. 54). Interestingly, in the 2007 survey, 20 per cent of primaries and 9 per cent of secondaries reported that they had no collaborative arrangements with other schools and that, in the future, for a variety of reasons, it is very likely that the traditional model will become increasingly unsustainable. However, as will be shown later, the traditional model is still the dominant one.

The second model identified – *a managed model* – had a flatter structure and specific roles allocated to senior support staff including directors of finance (bursar or school business leader) and/or human resources (HR). There was a more diverse SLT with consequently a greater degree of distributed leadership. Co-headship arrangements where the responsibilities can be split between two or more people in a variety of ways were a distinct subset of the managed model. Shared leadership as a means of making the role of headteacher more 'doable' was mentioned spontaneously by many respondents in the 2007 research who linked this approach to a more businesslike approach with a clear division of responsibilities. 'At times, this was linked with a move towards a 'Chief Operating Officer' model' (p. 59). The report claimed the managed model was becoming more common in the secondary sector with 'nearly half of secondary heads (46%) stated that they had one senior support staff member on the leadership team and a further 8% had two senior support staff members' (p. 55). In contrast, only about one in eight primary schools had a support staff member on the senior team and only one in fifty had two.

The third model, a *multi-agency managed* model, had an inter-agency focus with both teaching staff and professionals from other agencies on the SLT. This model was very much an extension of the managed model and was considered to be a variant rather than a completely separate model. It was characterized by 'a greater degree of multi-agency working and a more diverse workforce based on the school premises, including greater professional diversity in the SLT and, potentially, the governing body' (p. 61). This model remained uncommon but the report notes that 'as the extended services agenda becomes more embedded in schools we might expect many managed schools of all types to increasingly come to resemble the multi-agency model described here' (p. 61). However, the extended services and ECM agendas were replaced as policy priorities by the coalition government in 2010 and with the growth of partnership working and school collaboratives other models are likely to take its place.

The *federated* model was characterized by varying degrees of collaboration between schools. The 2007 study notes that with the introduction of the ECM and 14–19 policy agendas, it was clear that one school was unable to deliver all services and curricular requirements on their own. It was claimed these initiatives were leading to more consistent and formal collaborations between schools and other organizations. The federated model includes confederations and joint strategic governing bodies with an executive head but federated models do not necessarily preclude other models of leadership within the constituent schools. There are a number of leadership models dependent on the extent to which the schools within the federation are linked. About one-in-ten heads reported having some form of federative arrangement, while just under two-thirds reported a loose, informal collaboration with other schools. It was noted that:

There is no real difference in the types of school involved in federated arrangements, however, secondary schools are more likely to be involved in informal, loose collaborations than primary (67% compared to 61% respectively). Primary schools are more likely to have no collaborative arrangements at all (20% compared to 9% for secondary schools). (PwC, 2007, p. 77)

Unsurprisingly perhaps, a crucial factor affecting levels of involvement in collaboratives was the degree of perceived benefit to their schools.

The fifth model of school leadership from the 2007 study was that of *system leadership*, with the headteacher taking on a number of roles beyond the school to contribute to the wider system. As the National College explains system leadership is 'a new form of leadership which focuses the energies of school leaders not just on leading within their own schools, but beyond their schools on behalf of the wider system within their locality and beyond' (NCSL, 2006b, p. x). System leadership models include all the different roles that heads can assume beyond the boundaries of the school, that is, those that contribute to the wider educational system at a national, regional or local level. The 2007 report notes the range of forms this model can take including: consultant leaders; executive heads or teams of heads working with less successful schools; national leaders of education (NLEs); and new forms of leadership such as 'virtual heads' in response to specific circumstances. There is now a considerable literature on system leadership, consultant leaders, NLEs and National Support Schools (e.g. Earley and Weindling, 2006; Higham et al., 2009; Hill and Matthews, 2008, 2010; Ofsted 2011b) and since the publication of the 2007 report their numbers have steadily increased. In early 2013 there were approximately 800 NLEs, 2,000 Local Leaders of Education and 50 National Leaders of Governance.

The 2007 report concluded by noting that their five 'high level leadership models' of school leadership describe some of the existing, emerging and new models identified at the time of their research but that they are broad categories and there were found to be a large number of local variations on these themes or models. The five models are necessarily broad and not mutually exclusive. It also concluded by identifying a number of legal and regulatory barriers to implementing new models, for example, the roles and responsibilities of deputy heads and the extent to which they should be required to stand-in for heads.

The 2012 landscape report

So how have things changed since the 2007 report? The PwC survey did not ask questions using the five models of school leadership – they emerged out of the research findings. Neither did the 2012 leadership landscape report use these models for its survey of school leaders. Of course, with the change of government in 2010, the policy context had changed considerably between the times of the two surveys although there were still some policy continuities: considerable emphasis was still given to schools working together, partnership and collaboration. The period between the two surveys had also seen the further growth of different types of schools and forms of governance such as academies and chains (see Hill et al., 2012).

In the 2012 survey of the leadership landscape, headteachers were asked what was their current role or title. The result was that the traditional model or approach to headship – of one school, one headteacher – was still most prevalent. This was shown to be the predominant model for the vast majority (91%) of over 800 survey respondents (see Table 4.1). Relatedly, over eight out of ten headteachers (83%) described their institutional governance as a single stand alone school governing body (which could include an informal partnership) (see Table 4.2). There was also evidence, however, of the more recent growth of executive headship models – PwC's federated model – which were reported in 7 per cent of schools responding to the survey. The 2011 School Workforce Census (SWC) identified 410 executive heads (see Chapter 3.) Nearly one-in-ten schools was part of a hard federation – with one governing body across two or more schools – one in twenty was part of a collaborative (a soft or non-governance federation) and just 1 per cent was part of an academy chain. Two per cent of respondents reported that they were job-sharing one school's headship (co-headship – a subset of PwC's managed model of leadership) (Earley et al., 2012, pp. 66–7).

At the time of the 2012 survey, very few headteachers' schools were part of an academy chain (see Table 4.2) but 8 per cent were planning to become an academy. Of course both leadership surveys were conducted at particular points in time and reflect the situation at that time. Since the most recent

TABLE 4.1 Headship model of institution

Which of the following headship models best describes your institution?	%
Traditional (one headteacher, one school)	91
Two headteachers, job sharing one school's headship	2
One executive head of 2 or more schools, who directly leads each school	5
One executive head of 2 or more schools but with Heads of School responsible for the daily leadership of each school	2
Chief executive (or equivalent) of a chain of schools, with a Principal/Head responsible for the daily leadership of one	0
N = 833	

Note: A single response item. The percentages in this table are weighted by school type and FSM. Due to rounding, percentages may not sum to 100.
Source: Earley et al., 2012, p. 67.

TABLE 4.2 Governance structure of institution

Which of the following governance structures best describes your institution?	%
Stand alone (including informal partnership)	83
Part of a collaborative (e.g. soft or non-governance federation)	5
Part of a hard federation (one governing body)	9
Part of an academy chain	1
N = 833	

Note: A single response item. The percentages in this table are weighted by school type and FSM. Due to rounding, percentages may not sum to 100.
Source: Earley et al., 2012, p. 67.

survey for example that took place in early 2012, the growth of academies has been phenomenal. As of October 2012, there were 2,373 academies representing just over 10 per cent of the nation's schools, up from only 203 in September 2010, meaning that 2,170 schools had become academies in two years. Over that period the number of 'sponsored' academies had risen from 203 to 477 and the number of 'converter' academies from 0 to 1,896. By January 2013, nearly one-half of secondary schools nationally were academies but only about 5 per cent of primary schools (which represent over a third [34%] of the total number of academies). Academy-sponsored chains are a growing, if still small, part of the leadership landscape (see Hill et al., 2012). The coalition government continues to encourage schools to become academies – a policy that has not been without its critics.

Senior leadership teams

The 2012 landscape study gathered information on SLTs. The survey of headteachers found the average number of senior leaders serving in a school's core SLT was four (ranging from 0 to 15 members). The size and composition of the SLT were linked to the size, phase and context of the school. The previous chapter drew upon SWC data to document the size of SLTs in primary, secondary and special schools (see Table 3.1) and noted that there was relatively little variation in leadership teams by school governance type. Academies tend to have slightly larger leadership teams overall and voluntary-controlled schools the smallest, largely because the latter include many small rural primary schools.

Sixty-two per cent of headteachers reported there had been no change to the size of their current SLT in the past 12 months, while for one in five it had increased. Where the number had been increased, this was often in response to developments such as becoming a Teaching School or converting to an academy. Where the numbers had decreased, this was often due to financial pressures or an inherited 'top-heavy' structure. Nearly three-quarters (73%) had no plans to change the size over the next 12 months with about one-in-ten stating it was likely to decrease in size. For 14 per cent the SLT size was likely to increase.

Secondary school teams were larger and they were more likely to have plans to widen SLT membership in comparison to primary schools. These findings are broadly similar to those of the 2012 National College annual survey (BMG Research, 2012) which asked over 1,400 heads and deputy/assistant heads if their SLT was larger, smaller or the same size compared to the same time last year. The size of the SLT was largely unchanged. Where SLTs were smaller, this was largely due to retirement or staff having left and not been replaced (37%) or as a result of reduced funding (31%).

Within the 2012 landscape survey, just over a third (37%) of headteachers reported that they had appointed a bursar or school business manager (SBM) onto the SLT (59% of the schools in the sample had one). This was the case in 71 per cent of secondary schools but was true of only 30 per cent of primary schools – a statistically significant difference.

There was therefore some evidence of the 2007 report's managed models with a more diverse SLT and specific roles allocated to senior support staff including school business managers and/or directors of HR. In all but the smallest schools the school business manager was usually included in the team. Less frequently, another senior member of the school's support staff was also included. Unlike the 2007 study however, little or no reference was made to multi-agency working which was probably a reflection of the change of policy direction from 2010. Where recent restructuring of SLT roles had taken place there was often a focus on improving teaching and learning. As well as staff on the leadership scale, such as deputy or assistant headteachers, a majority of the SLTs in the 2012 case studies included other teachers who were seen as key to improvements in teaching and learning, such as subject leaders for core subjects and/or Advanced Skills Teachers (Earley et al., 2012, pp. 67–8).

Approaches to leadership

The 2012 study also included a survey of senior/middle leaders who were asked about their school's approach to leadership. As Table 4.3 demonstrates, leadership strategies were commonly being adopted that encouraged a more

TABLE 4.3 Information about leadership strategies – middle/senior leaders and Heads (given in parentheses)

Leadership strategies					
To what extent has your school used the following strategies on leadership?	We have been doing this for a year or more (%)	Yes in the last 12 months (%)	Plan to do so in the next 12 months (%)	No current plans to do so (%)	No response (%)
Widened SLT membership	44 (23)	25 (22)	5 (12)	24 (40)	3 (2)
Built a flatter less hierarchical leadership structure and ethos	36 (38)	22 (23)	6 (8)	31 (28)	4 (3)
Encouraged and enabled teachers to contribute to school leadership	50 (52)	32 (37)	5 (9)	11 (1)	2 (1)
Shared specific leadership responsibilities with a partner or across a family of schools	18 (14)	15 (14)	12 (16)	51 (55)	4 (1)
Developed an Executive Head and Head of School model	6 (5)	3 (1)	4 (3)	81 (88)	6 (2)
N = 769 senior/middle leaders (N = 834 Headteachers)					

Note: A series of single response items. Percentages in brackets are from the headteacher survey. The percentages in this table are weighted by school type, size and FSM. Due to rounding, percentages may not sum to 100.
Source: Earley et al., 2012, p. 69.

collective or distributed approach to leadership. For example, 69 per cent of respondents reported that their school had widened its SLT membership. Fifty-eight per cent said that a flatter less hierarchical leadership structure had been developed within their school. Eighty-two per cent of the senior/middle leaders stated that contributions to school leadership from teachers had been encouraged. The comparable figures from the 2012 headteacher survey are shown in brackets in Table 4.3.

More diverse SLTs and flatter leadership structures with greater degrees of distributed leadership, as outlined in the 2007 report's managed model, appeared to be quite commonplace in 2012. However, there were several school phase and type differences:

- Primary school respondents were more likely to report the adoption of a flatter leadership structure than other schools. Academy respondents were more likely to respond that their school had no current plans to introduce less hierarchical structures.

- Respondents from schools categorized by Ofsted as 'satisfactory' ('requires improvement') or 'poor' were less likely to answer that teachers had been encouraged to contribute to school leadership 'in the last 12 months'.

There was also evidence that shared leadership strategies, in partnership with other schools, were developing. While one-half (51%) of middle/senior leader respondents reported their school had no plans to share leadership responsibilities with a partner or across a family of schools, one-third were already doing so. Further, while 81 per cent had no current plans to develop an executive head and head of school model, 9 per cent were already doing so (6% for more than a year). This mirrors the existence of executive headship – or the federated model – within some schools. Interestingly, nearly nine-out-of-ten headteachers (88%) stated they had no current plans to develop such a model. There is a broad similarity in survey responses across the various sets of respondents, although it should be noted that the headteachers and middle/senior leaders were not necessarily from the same schools (Earley et al., 2012, pp. 68–9).

Heads' views on middle leaders

In the 2012 landscape study, interview and case study participants commonly described how building a culture that supports leadership at all levels and sharing a vision for doing this was an important part of the role of the headteacher. Senior leaders often reported that they needed to continue to develop shared responsibility and accountability for outcomes among all staff. The need to develop the ability of colleagues to cope with uncertainty and change in a shifting policy climate was also reported (Earley et al., 2012, p. 69).

Differences emerged between primary and secondary schools concerning middle leadership. Primary headteachers referred to the sharing of leadership roles across the school and staffs' willingness to take on extra responsibility even where there was no formal pay or status recognition for this. Most primary school teachers had subject coordination responsibilities. Teachers with teaching and learning responsibility points (TLRs) were usually included within the SLT of small schools. Primary heads usually considered leadership to be good and developing at all levels, with the main area identified for development relating to the roles of support staff.

A mixed picture was more frequently reported in secondary schools where heads expressed concerns about middle leadership (heads of department and faculty), including in the core subjects of English, mathematics and science. A number of strategies for monitoring and improving middle leadership were reported by headteachers. These included:

- Line management, for example, with senior leaders monitoring closely pupil progress and the impact of interventions in a specific department;

- Performance management, including formal or informal capability measures, individual improvement plans;

- Using 'mini-inspections' of subject areas, by internal or external colleagues;

- Use of leadership development programmes, such as those from the National College. These were often run locally in a partnership arrangement or in house;

- Using support from other schools, for example, with the head of department from another school supporting directly the respective subject leader;

- Restructuring, for instance in one case using an AST (Advanced Skills Teacher) to lead teaching and learning in a core subject area with an SLT member leading departmental management. (Earley et al., 2012, p. 70)

Recruitment of senior and middle leaders

The 2012 headteacher survey asked respondents about the recruitment of senior and middle leaders. About one in eight schools (13%) reported challenges currently in recruiting senior and middle leaders. There were no significant differences between school types or phases.

Headteachers were also asked about the factors impacting upon the recruitment and retention of both senior and middle leaders. As can be seen in Table 4.4, about one quarter (26%) reported that a lack of credible external candidates for senior leadership posts (as opposed to 17% for internal candidates) had impacted 'significantly' or 'a lot' on recruitment and retention. The most significant factor, however, was changes to the school budget. Thirty per cent of headteachers reported this impacted 'very significantly', 17 per cent 'a lot' and 22 per cent 'partially'.

Several significant differences by school phase and type were found:

- Headteachers of schools with an above average number of children entitled to Free School Meals (FSM) were *most* likely to consider a lack of credible external middle leader candidates to be 'very significant'.

- Secondary school, special school and PRU headteachers were *least* likely to respond 'not at all' on whether a lack of external credible candidates for middle leader posts impacted on their school. (Earley et al., 2012, p. 71)

Recruitment difficulties

School leadership recruitment difficulties have existed throughout the period of this study. In 2002, for example, respondents were of the view that recruitment and retention of school leaders was likely to become increasingly problematic. As a response to these continuing recruitment difficulties it was recommended in the 2007 report that those without classroom experience or qualified teacher status (QTS) be permitted to lead schools, provided there was a senior qualified teacher who was a member of the SLT. The 2007 report also noted the pay differentials between headship and deputy headship and between senior leadership and the highest paid teachers were insufficient. The attractiveness of headship was being affected by increased workload which, it was suggested, could be resolved either by a greater distribution of responsibilities among the SLT or by increasing salaries.

The declining attractiveness of headship has also been raised in other studies. The National College (2006) found almost one-third of primary and

TABLE 4.4 Factors impacting upon recruitment and retention of senior and middle leaders

Recruitment and retention of middle/senior leaders						
Do the following factors impact on recruitment and retention?	Very significantly (%)	A lot (%)	Partially (%)	Very little (%)	Not at all (%)	No response (%)
Lack of credible candidates for senior leadership posts externally	13	13	21	12	34	7
Lack of credible candidates for senior leadership posts internally	7	10	18	17	42	7
Lack of credible candidates for middle leadership posts externally	7	11	26	13	35	8
Lack of credible candidates for middle leadership posts internally	5	7	18	21	42	8
Changes to your school budget	30	17	22	8	16	7
N = 833						

Note: A series of single response items. The percentages in this table are weighted by school type and FSM. Due to rounding, percentages may not sum to 100.
Source: Earley et al., 2012, p. 72.

secondary headships were re-advertised because there was no suitable candidate. This was partly due to demography with nearly a quarter of headteachers aged over 55 and predicted to retire over the next five years. Also there was a lower than average number of teachers in the following generation from which new school leaders would normally emerge. Smithers and Robinson (2007) were surprised there was a secondary headteacher shortage as the average teacher:headteacher ratio was 60:1. In primary schools a shortage was more likely as it was 10:1. They also proposed a range of other important non-demographic factors such as workload, excessive accountability, too many government initiatives, vulnerability to dismissal through poor inspection reports and insufficient salary differentials.

Difficulties in the recruitment and retention of school leaders, especially headteachers, has led to a number of initiatives and developments in talent management, accelerated leadership development and in succession planning – notably the National College's local solutions approach (Earley and Jones, 2010; Davies and Davies, 2011; Fink, 2010).

Leadership challenges

Having considered changing models and leadership structures, the second part of this chapter examines the most significant challenges faced by school leaders and briefly compares these challenges with those mentioned in earlier studies of leadership. Leadership challenges were not a central focus of the original 2002 baseline study, although the follow-up study in 2005 conducted some online focus groups to gather some illustrative qualitative data on this theme. The following were mentioned as significant challenges being faced by heads in the mid-2000s:

- Managing new initiatives and complying with new legislation – sifting through the most important and relevant for each school, its staff and children.

- Raising school achievement – not necessarily achieving exam targets.

- Pupil behaviour.

- Workforce reform and workload – no central funding yet the challenge remained to sustain the changes.

- Unique challenges for small schools – less money, fewer teachers.

- Inclusion – accommodating pupils with Special Educational Needs (SEN) in mainstream without adequate provision.

- Gaining cooperation of a wide variety of providers so individual needs of young people were met. (Stevens et al., 2005, p. xxi)

Two years later the 2007 report showed that school leaders were facing a variety of similar challenges and issues but in an ever-changing landscape. The challenges they reported to be facing were wide ranging and included raising and maintaining standards (15%), followed by pupil attainment, achievement and results (10%), staff improvement and development (7%) and recruiting and retaining the workforce (7%). Work-life balance issues, dealing with government initiatives and ensuring a personalized learning environment were also noted (PwC, 2007, p. 14).

In the 2012 landscape study, headteachers, governors and senior/middle leaders were asked to describe the three most significant challenges they anticipated facing over the next 18 months (Earley et al., 2012, pp. 74–8). There is likely to be a relationship between role responsibility and perceived challenges in leadership but across all three sets of respondents the most common concern was funding. Forty-four per cent of headteachers, 34 per cent of governors and 24 per cent of senior/middle leaders anticipated finance/budget issues and/or reductions in funding/austerity measures as a key leadership challenge. Comments on this challenge included: 'doing more with fewer resources', 'managing a reducing school budget', 'coping with funding reductions', 'dealing with the financial situation – implementing cuts', 'dealing with potential budget decreases', and 'managing the finance with a significantly reducing roll and significant decrease in budget allocation'. An example of how one of the case study schools was considering funding and pupil numbers is given below.

Case study: A perspective on funding and pupil numbers

A mixed 11–16 school with approximately 1,000 students had been judged by Ofsted in 2009 to be a 'satisfactory' school. The school had an above average number of students eligible for Free School Meals. Recently, the school had become an academy as a partner to a local 'outstanding' school converting to academy status.

The school had experienced a significant budget decline after a number of partnership grants on behaviour and extended schooling ended in 2010. The school started a natural wastage (non-replacement of staff) process in 2011 and this had saved £290,000. The funding challenge was also demographic. While local infant and nursery provision were experiencing an expanding student cohort, the secondary phase had a significantly smaller than average cohort. The larger younger cohort was expected locally to feed into secondary schools in 5–7 years.

This had led the principal to start

'a marketing splurge on the back of our move to academy status . . . I've been playing hardball with the advertisements, much to the annoyance of local heads, but that's the name of the game . . . We needed to change the image of the school – through direct advertisements, newspapers, radio, getting into primary schools through liaison and targeting schools that you know have large cohorts in the primary phase . . . This has been even to the detriment of some primary heads [in the neighbouring Authority] getting letters . . . forbidding them having any conversation with me'.

In 2011/12, the Year 7 intake had increased by 15 students to take the year group 'back up to 202'. A similar increase in 2012/13 would equate to an additional £150,000 from increased student funding. This led the principal to 'believe we cannot be significantly damaged by falling rolls'.

Source: Earley et al., 2012, p. 76.

In addition to funding, other challenges faced by school leaders in 2012 were:

- The new Ofsted inspection framework: a concern for 26 per cent of heads, 13 per cent of chairs of governors and 22 per cent of senior/middle leaders.

- Academy status: a concern for 16 per cent of heads, 25 per cent of governors and 8 per cent of senior/middle leaders.

- Sustaining/improving student outcomes (attainment): a concern for 18 per cent of heads, 10 per cent of governors and 18 per cent of senior/middle leaders.

- Staff recruitment and retention: a concern for 15 per cent of heads, 18 per cent of governors (regarding the head/deputy head) and 10 per cent of senior/middle leaders.

- Admissions/pupil numbers (impact of falling roll/oversubscription/competition from other schools): a concern for 10 per cent of heads and 13 per cent of governors.

- Curriculum changes/introduction of new National Curriculum: a concern for 10 per cent of heads and 11 per cent of senior/middle leaders.

- The rapid pace of policy change (coping with/keeping staff informed): a concern for 9 per cent of both heads and senior/middle leaders.

- Change/reduction in LA support (minimising impact/managing without/leading to rural isolation): a concern for 9 per cent of heads and 8 per cent of senior/middle leaders.

- Sustaining/building on/moving to an 'outstanding' judgement: a concern for 11 per cent of governors and 6 per cent of senior/middle leaders.

- Improving/maintaining/developing collaborative links with other schools – (including Trust status): a concern for 11 per cent of governors and 5 per cent of senior/middle leaders.

Surprisingly few respondents directly identified improving the quality of teaching and learning as being a key leadership challenge. Among senior/middle leaders, 5 per cent did include staff development and 9 per cent tackling underperformance of staff as key challenges.

The National College's 2012 annual survey of school leaders (BMG Research, 2012) provides interesting comparable data regarding current challenges. Improving pupil/student achievement/standards remained headteachers' main priority (37% compared with 35% in the 2011 College annual survey). Schools judged 'satisfactory' by Ofsted were found to be more likely to mention improving pupil/student achievement/standards than 'outstanding' and 'good' schools. Headteachers' other priorities were improving teaching standards (31%), staff development (16%) and preparation for the new Ofsted framework (14%). 'Managing funding/financial management/setting balanced budgets' was mentioned by only 9 per cent of headteachers in 2012, with primary heads less likely to mention this factor. In the earlier College annual survey of 2011 this figure was much higher (27%) – similar to that found in Earley et al. (2012). It is not clear, however, why such a difference existed between the two studies or between the two years of the National College's annual survey. Managing finance and budgets is always likely to be a challenge at a time of financial austerity (Earley et al., 2012, p. 79).

Summary

This chapter has drawn upon the various leadership studies from 2002 to 2012 to consider the key themes of leadership models and challenges. It drew predominantly upon the 2007 study and the most recent study of the leadership landscape in 2012 to examine roles and approaches, including the senior leadership team (SLT) and middle leadership; leadership recruitment and retention; and the most significant leadership challenges currently faced and anticipated in the near future.

Regarding leadership models in schools, the traditional approach to headship – of one school, one headteacher – was still the predominant model in 2012. On school governance structures over eight out of ten headteachers described their institution as 'stand alone'. The more recent growth of executive headship or federated models was also reflected in the data. Nearly one-in-ten was part of a hard federation, which reflects but is not limited to the growth in executive headship – a form of system leadership. The average number of senior leaders serving in a school's core SLT in 2012 was four, with just under two-thirds, mostly primary schools, not having a bursar or school business manager on the team.

In the 2012 study there was a trend, earlier identified in the 2007 study, towards flatter, less hierarchical leadership structures and contributions to school leadership were often encouraged from teachers. Primary schools had flatter leadership arrangements than other schools and academies were less likely to have plans to introduce less hierarchical structures.

On key leadership challenges, the main concern in the 2012 study was monetary, with nearly half of headteachers, a third of chairs of governors and a quarter of senior/middle leaders making reference to finance/budget issues and reductions in funding/austerity measures. Surprisingly, improving the quality of teaching and learning was not commonly mentioned specifically as being a key leadership challenge although improving student outcomes was a concern for nearly a fifth of heads and senior/middle leaders. In the 2012 National College annual survey, improving pupil/student achievement/ standards remained the main priority of headteachers.

5

Governing Bodies

Introduction

Given the policy changes over the last decade or so, the role of school governance is of increasing significance. The governing body represents an important element of school leadership; it is the strategic, accountable body for the school. Governing bodies and their role in school improvement has always been important (e.g. Scanlon et al., 1999; Creese and Earley, 1999) but it has increased in the light of policy developments. The potential increase in school autonomy from Local Authority (LA) governance, through the adoption of academy status or through other clustering arrangements and formal federations, may well place new duties and pressures on school governors as well as potentially changing who is governing. Policy change is adding new complexity to the governor role, with governors having to keep abreast of policy, legal duties and changing external landscapes that can affect the strategic direction of their school (James, 2011). This will test governing body capability. Policies that increase school autonomy in corporate matters also encourage the need for corporate capacity within the governing body, given the importance of raising issues relevant to probity and value for money in institutions without other local democratic oversight.

Governance has also been shown to be a key site where new actors such as businesses, charities and faith groups are working within the state and thus where the boundaries between the state, private and voluntary sectors is becoming increasingly blurred (Ball, 2009). In this context, monitoring and ensuring responsiveness to local needs and interests may also become more significant, especially where this has been a key concern for protests against adopting academy status (Curtis et al., 2008; Chitty, 2011).

Notwithstanding these rapid changes, the central role of school governors in England, regardless of their position in the sector, remains their responsibility for the school and school improvement (Earley and Weindling, 2004). Research suggests that the quality of the governing body is an important influence on school improvement (Balarin et al., 2008; Dean et al., 2007; Ranson et al., 2005). The chair of the governing body needs to be able to negotiate and manage a productive as well as a challenging stance with the headteacher (Ranson, 2008; James, 2011). However, evidence suggests that the governor role tends towards scrutiny activity rather than a sustained focus and appraisal of improvement and effectiveness in schools (Ranson, 2008; James, 2011). Certainly an ineffective governing body does appear to have a demonstrable negative impact on outcomes; particularly where there are low levels of governor capacity and competence (Scanlon et al., 1999; Earley, 2003; Balarin et al., 2008; James, 2011; Ofsted, 2011a). Ofsted notes that an effective governing body is:

> characterised by a collective ambition for the school to excel. The governors provide a good balance between supporting the school and ensuring that ambitious targets for improvement are set and achieved. They are fully informed and are able to ask challenging questions about the work of the school; thereby holding leaders and managers to account. (Ofsted, 2012a, p. 16)

The governor role is then significant to leadership both in terms of the scale of volunteering or sponsoring and the influence on school improvement, even though the traditional governor contribution is not always acknowledged (James, 2011). Concerns have been raised about the capacity of volunteers to defend the school rigorously, challenge for improvement and be a critical friend, especially with a self-improving school-led system (Balarin et al., 2008; James et al., 2011). The notion of system leadership has been extended to governors, with chairs of governing bodies asked to put themselves forward for assessment as National Leaders of Governance (NLGs). By the end of 2012 there were over 50 NLGs.

This chapter considers the role of school governing bodies within the changing leadership landscape drawing upon data from the leadership baseline studies. In so doing we are able to see where governors are involved in leadership activities and how things have changed or remained the same over time. It begins, however, by providing some basic information about the composition of school governing bodies in 2012 before considering their leadership role, how governors' and headteachers' perceptions of this have changed over time, their training and development needs and their views on the education policy landscape.

Governing bodies – demographic and other information

The 2012 landscape survey showed that the average number of governors serving on a school governing body was 14. If there were no vacancies the mean size of the full governing body was reported to be 15. On changes to the size and membership of the governing body, 72 per cent of chairs of governors and 64 per cent of heads reported there had been no recent change. Three-quarters of both groups reported there were no planned changes to the size of the governing body for the next 12 months. Further analysis showed that secondary school heads were most likely to report the governing body size was likely to decrease over the next year (Earley et al., 2012, p. 72).

On recruiting governors, over a third of chairs of governors (38%) and nearly one-half (47%) of heads reported experiencing difficulties over the last 12 months. Governor recruitment was more difficult in schools in challenging areas (high free school meals [FSM]), a finding noted consistently by other leadership studies including the 2005 study, with parent, community and foundation governors more likely to be unfilled vacancies. Among the factors impacting on the recruitment and retention of governors, chairs of governors reported in 2012 that low volunteering rates (32%), increasing time commitments (30%) and heavy workloads (20%) were 'very significant' or impacted 'a lot'. Schools had used a number of strategies to address governor recruitment difficulties. These included approaching directly potential candidates (72%), advertising in the school newsletter (65%) and working with the LA (45%). Despite voicing difficulty in recruiting to their governing body, the vast majority of chairs of governors (92%) were confident that their governing body had the skills to recruit and appoint a replacement headteacher. Also most (71%) believed they would be able to find and recruit a high quality replacement (Earley et al., 2012, p. 72).

Until 2012 in England the possession of the National Professional Qualification for Headship (NPQH) was a requirement for appointment as a headteacher. In the 2012 survey, governor attitudes towards NPQH were generally positive with only 1 per cent of chairs noting that they would not expect candidates to have the qualification when recruiting for a head. However, 40 per cent were not aware of the change to the requirement to possess NPQH. Further, a great majority of chairs (89%) said they would support staff who wished to undertake NPQH for professional development.

The 2012 survey also asked chairs of governors how many hours they spent on various governor-related tasks in a typical month. Chairs, who usually spend more time on gubernatorial matters than other governors (Scanlon et al., 1999), on average spent 22 hours per month with most time spent in committees and other meetings (5 hours a month, although this ranged from 1 to 35 hours, as shown in Table 5.1). They also spent an average of four hours a month working directly with the headteacher and preparing for meetings (again, the range of time spent on such tasks was considerable). Further analysis showed that chairs from schools graded 'outstanding' by inspectors tended to spend fewer hours than chairs from other schools on most of these tasks (but not committees or preparation and paperwork for governing body meetings).

Chairs of governors were also asked which activities, including those relating to partnership working, they had personally undertaken as a governor (at their own school or elsewhere). As can be seen from Table 5.2, nearly three-quarters (72%) had helped to recruit a headteacher, while a fifth (19%) had worked to support a governing body at another school. Levels of governor involvement in various leadership activities is considered in the next section.

TABLE 5.1 Time spent every month on tasks – chairs of governors

	Valid N	Minimum	Mean	Maximum
In committees and other meetings	338	1	5	35
Working directly with the headteacher/principal	339	0	4	30
Working with the bursar/ school business manager	256	0	2	25
With pupils and students	269	0	2	15
With parents	244	0	1	10
Training	269	0	2	15
Working with teachers and other school staff	283	0	2	12
Preparation and paperwork for governing body meetings	334	0	4	30

Source: Earley et al., 2012, p. 85.

TABLE 5.2 Activities undertaken by chairs of governors

Which of the following activities have you personally undertaken as a governor (at your current school or elsewhere)?	%
Recruited and appointed a headteacher/principal	72
Chaired an interim executive board/ temporary governing body	14
Chaired the academy sponsorship process	5
Chaired/or been involved in the process of an academy conversion	16
Chaired/or been involved in the creation of a Federation of schools	14
Worked to support a governing body at another school	19
Chaired the establishment of formal collaboration with another school	10
Chaired the development of an informal partnership with another school	15
No response	15
N = 347	

Note: More than one answer could be put forward so percentages may sum to more than 100. The percentages in this table are weighted by school type and FSM. Due to rounding, percentages may not sum to 100.
Source: Earley et al., 2012, p. 90.

In an open-ended question, chairs of governors and heads were asked to list the three most significant leadership challenges they anticipated facing over the next 18 months and these were discussed in the previous chapter. The top three listed by chairs were to do with finance or budgetary issues; issues around academy status; and appointing senior staff. Interestingly the fourth most mentioned area was about improving or empowering the governing body. It is to their roles in leadership, especially strategic leadership that we now turn.

Governing bodies and leadership

The school governing body's role is often conceptualized in terms of three main functions: providing critical friendship to the head and senior staff, ensuring accountability and helping to bring about change and improvement through such activities as monitoring and evaluating the work of the school.

The governing body is an important element of strategic leadership and is the accountable body for the school. The perceived degree of governing body involvement in strategic leadership is one of the few areas that have been examined consistently over the course of the three leadership studies with similar questions being asked in the 2002, 2005 and 2012 surveys. (However, whereas the first and second surveys were of governors, the most recent study involved chairs of governors only.)

On the role that the governing body *should* play as opposed to the role it *does* play in strategic leadership, there was, perhaps unsurprisingly, a disparity between headteacher and chair of governor views. This was found to be the case for all three surveys. As Tables 5.3 and 5.4 demonstrate, in the 2012 survey, 79 per cent of chairs of governors believed that the governing body *should* have a major role in the school's strategic leadership, but this was the case for only 46 per cent of headteachers. (It should be noted that governor and headteacher respondents may have come from different schools. This is true of all three leadership studies.)

Similarly, while 46 per cent of chairs of governors in the 2012 survey stated that the governing body *does* play a major role in strategic leadership, only 22 per cent of headteachers believed this was the case. Exactly one-half of headteachers believed governors played a moderate role and just over a quarter (26%) believed governors played only a minor role.

These discrepant views between governors and headteachers may relate to the difficulty noted by leaders in recruiting to their governing body and/or the difference in perceptions and expectations of the role. As noted above, chairs of governors suggested difficulty in recruitment may be due to low volunteering rates, increasing time commitments and heavy governor workload; the extent of which may not be acknowledged by headteachers who believe that governors should be playing a *more* significant role.

Overall, however, the 2012 figures compare favourably with those collected earlier in the baseline study of 2002 and that of 2005. Of course the differences (improvements) could be because the 2012 survey respondents were chairs and not just governors and therefore perhaps they were likely to see themselves as being more involved in strategic leadership than the average member. For the purpose of comparison, Tables 5.3 and 5.4 include (in brackets) the percentage figures on the Likert scale for the 2002 and 2005 surveys. Both headteachers and governors reported greater governor involvement in school leadership in 2012 than in either 2005 or 2002 which may reflect the greater importance accorded to governors over this period and as schools have become more autonomous and have greater control over their resources. Governors were consistently much more likely to see themselves as playing a major or moderate strategic leadership role than were headteachers. The vast majority of governors also believed that their

TABLE 5.3 Role of governors in strategic leadership: Headteacher responses

Role of governors in strategic leadership – headteachers 2012, (2005) and [2002]				
	Major role %	Moderate role %	Minor role %	No role at all %	%
Role it *should* play	46 (32) [22]	43 (54) [58]	8 (12) [18]	2 (1) [2.5]	1
Role it *actually* plays	22 (17) [13]	50 (50) [52]	26 (29) [31]	1 (3) [0]	1

Note: A series of single response items. The percentages in this table are weighted by school type and FSM, Due to rounding, percentages may not sum to 100. Figures in brackets are taken from Stevens et al., (2005) and Earley et al., [2002]
N = 833 (2012); N = 911 (2005); N = 608 [2002].
Source: Earley et al., 2012, p. 73.

TABLE 5.4 Role of governors in strategic leadership: Chairs of governor responses

Role of governors in strategic leadership – Chairs of Governors 2012 and Governors (2005) and [2002]				
	Major role %	Moderate role %	Minor role %	No role at all %
Role it *should* play	79 (66) [57]	21 (31) [39]	0 (1) [4]	0 (0) [0]
Role it *actually* plays	46 (40) [29]	50 (52) [56]	4 (6) [15]	0 (0.5) [0]

Note: A series of single response items. The percentages in this table are weighted by school type and FSM. Due to rounding, percentages may not sum to 100. Figures in brackets are taken from Stevens et al., (2005) and Earley et al., [2002].
N = 347 (2012); N = 479; (2005); N = 197 [2002].
NB 2012 survey = chairs of governors; 2005 and 2002 surveys = governors
Source: Earley et al., 2012, p. 74.

governing body's role in the leadership of their school was *very* or *fairly* significant.

The National College's annual survey of school leadership (BMG, 2012), which was completed at about the same time as the 2012 survey, asked headteachers (n = 837) how effective they considered their school's governing body to be in: providing effective challenge to the headteacher and the senior leadership team (SLT); understanding their strategic responsibilities; and driving school improvement as a whole. Headteachers stating that their governing body was 'very effective' in these three areas were, respectively, 51 per cent, 52 per cent and 42 per cent (Earley et al., 2012, p. 74). These figures indicate a reasonably high level of governing body effectiveness but as noted earlier it is those schools that would benefit most from an effective governing body that often may not have one.

Involvement in leadership tasks

The research findings indicate that headteachers recognize the importance of the governing body in having a leadership role within the school, offering support and challenge and holding the school's leadership to account for its performance. This role has been recognized in the most recent Ofsted inspection framework where the governing body is seen as an integral part of the school's leadership and management (Ofsted, 2012b). The governing body, or at least a subgroup of it, is also responsible (with help from an external adviser) for the performance management of the headteacher. As the leadership surveys demonstrate, the proportion of heads who see governing bodies having a major role in strategic leadership has grown significantly (from 22% to 46%) over the period, 2002–12. But what levels of involvement do governors have in the various areas of leadership? In the 2012 survey chairs of governors were asked to indicate the level of involvement of their governing body in a range of leadership areas. The findings are shown in Table 5.5.

As can be seen in Table 5.5, 'supporting the headteacher/principal to achieve the stated aims' of the school was the area that scored the highest with eight out of ten chairs of governors claiming that the governing body was 'very involved'. The next highest rating items were: monitoring the school budget and taking decisions to improve value for money (69%); monitoring and evaluating the school's progress in achieving its stated aims (68%); challenging the headteacher/principal to ensure the stated aims are achieved (67%); and helping to make key strategic decisions (64%). Governing bodies were less involved in the day-to-day running of the school or the professional development of staff. Interestingly, over one in five chairs (21%) were involved to some degree in mentoring and supporting governors in other schools. (It is not known how many of the sample were NLGs.)

School leader participants in the 2012 landscape study (in both the interviews and case studies) also commonly reported on the good working relations with their governing bodies, with a majority of governors said to be

TABLE 5.5 Involvement of governing body in leadership activities and tasks – chairs

How involved is the governing body in the following areas?	Very involved (%)	Quite involved (%)	Partially involved (%)	Very little (%)	Not at all involved (%)	No response (%)
Setting the aims and the objectives of the school	61	33	5	1	0	0
Setting policies for achieving school aims and objectives	55	37	6	0	0	0
Setting targets for achieving these aims and objectives	48	36	14	1	0	0
Monitoring and evaluating the school's progress in achieving its stated aims	68	28	4	0	0	0
Supporting the headteacher/ principal to achieve the stated aims	80	19	1	0	0	0
Challenging the headteacher/ principal to ensure the stated aims are achieved	67	26	5	1	0	1
Helping to make key strategic decisions	64	32	3	1	0	0
Monitoring the school budget and taking decisions to improve value for money	69	27	3	0	0	0

How involved is the governing body in the following areas?	Very involved (%)	Quite involved (%)	Partially involved (%)	Very little (%)	Not at all involved (%)	No response (%)
Actively considering any risks the school is facing	58	33	7	1	0	0
Building strong relations with the local community	32	39	24	4	0	1
Mentoring and supporting governors in other schools	3	7	11	32	46	0
Ensuring the day-to-day operation of the school is effective	23	33	26	14	4	0
Ensuring that school staff have the professional development and support they need to improve	24	37	27	10	1	0
Ensuring that succession plans are in place if the head teacher retires or is unable to work	32	36	18	11	3	1

N = 347

Note: A series of single response items. The percentages in this table are weighted by school type and FSM. Due to rounding, percentages may not sum to 100.
Source: Earley et al., 2012, p. 89.

involved and interested in the life of the school. Interviewed headteachers reported a high level of skills among their governors and were particularly appreciative of those who had themselves held senior posts in education and who had both time and expertise to offer to the school.

A minority of headteachers noted a relative lack of educational expertise among their governors and, because of this, an inability to provide suitable challenge on specific issues. A minority of governing bodies were also reported to need help in understanding the implications of the changing context in which they hold their responsibilities. (The chapter's final section considers governors' views of the current policy landscape.) One headteacher, for instance, ran regular governor meetings on teaching and learning, behaviour, human resources and admissions and also ran workshops for governors on, for instance, curriculum, assessment and planning to support their contribution to leadership and governance.

The 2012 survey responses and the qualitative data show that both headteachers and governors were in overall support for increasing the strategic leadership role of the governing body. Ensuring that this happens in practice is the challenge however. Increasing the provision of training and development programmes for governors in this specific area of leadership may be one way of improving the effectiveness of the governing body. Training and development is the focus of the next section.

Training and development for governors

Training and development for governors is not compulsory but is often seen as necessary if governors are to fulfil their duties effectively. The 2005 study reported that the amount of training governors received had influenced their perceptions of the effectiveness of the governing body. It noted that:

> Nine in ten governors who have had at least a fair amount of training (92%) feel that their governing body is effective in setting aims and objectives, compared with 85% of governors who have had hardly any training. Similarly governors who have had training for their role are more likely to perceive their governing body as effective in setting policies (92%), than those who have had hardly any training (83%). (Stevens et al., 2005, p. 118)

Governors who had more training were more likely to say that their governing body worked well with the headteacher in identifying and developing school management teams. They note 'Four in five governors who have had a fair amount or a great deal of training (82%) feel that their governing body works well with the headteacher in this aspect, compared with just seven in ten governors who have had hardly any training (70%)' (Stevens et al., 2005, p. 119). They also note, as did the 2002 baseline study, that governors in secondary schools felt more confident of the relationship between the governing body and the headteacher than governors of other schools. The 2005 study also noted a similar phase trend and found that one-fifth (21%) of heads in their survey described their governing body as quite or very ineffective which 'suggests that there is a need for capacity building measures for some governing bodies in order to provide the strategic challenge required' (p. 114). Ineffectiveness was often perceived by headteacher respondents in terms of governor inexperience, lack of skills and knowledge and little proactive support or involvement from the governing body.

About the same number referred to their governing body as effective. Effective governing bodies were seen as supportive of the head, good communicators, pragmatic and committed (see also Earley and Weindling, 2004; Scanlon et al., 1999). The 2007 study reported, as have most other studies of governing bodies, considerable variation in practice arguing that a more strategic approach to governance was required in the new school landscape. Interestingly, the 2007 study asked governors about the ways in which they could best support school leaders of the future. Their main response (23%) was to ensure that governors were fully trained/qualified/had a good understanding of the issues, with improved/closer working relationship with the headteacher (22%) close behind.

Strengthening the skills base of the governing body is important to manage the developing educational landscape in the context of greater school autonomy and accountability. Training and development is therefore a key matter. The 2012 landscape study found that the bulk of governing bodies (88%) had a budget for governor training and that three-quarters (73%) had conducted a governor skills audit over the last 18 months (30% in the last six months). The skills and qualities that chairs felt they needed to develop over the next 18 months are listed in Table 5.6 which shows the most reported areas to be developed as: building the capacity of the governing body (60%); preparing for the new Ofsted inspection framework (57%); and developing partnerships with other schools and agencies to improve outcomes (51%).

Strategic thinking and scanning the environment to anticipate future trends was recorded by over 40 per cent of chairs in the 2012 survey. Indeed, when asked in an open-ended question, how the strategic (SLT and governors) leadership of the school could be improved the most common response

TABLE 5.6 Leadership skills and qualities most needed over next 18 months – chairs

Governor development needs	
Which, if any, of the following skills and qualities do you think you most need to develop for yourself over the next 18 months?	%
Building the capacity of the governing body; developing skills and confidence	60
How to prepare for the new Ofsted inspection framework	57
Developing partnerships with other schools and agencies to improve outcomes	51
Overseeing change and improvement successfully	46
Supporting the development of effective relations with parents and the community	42
Strategic thinking and scanning to anticipate future trends	42
Monitoring the development of leadership succession planning	40
Understanding and interpreting student data and information	36
Knowing about key decisions in transitioning to Academy status	29
Managing the performance of the headteacher	28
Marketing your school	28
Knowing your legal responsibilities as a school governor	26
How to challenge and ask the right questions	26
Managing finances	25
$N = 347$	

Note: More than one answer could be put forward so percentages may sum to more than 100. The percentages in this table are weighted by school type and FSM. Due to rounding, percentages may not sum to 100.
Source: Earley et al., 2012, p. 105.

(mentioned by about one-in-ten of chair respondents to this question) was for more training and to develop expertise to help take the school forward.

Other suggestions included: opportunities to train together with the SLT, more time for training, greater involvement in key roles (such as monitoring and evaluation) and ensuring the governing body comprises a group of skilled and motivated people.

Where governors noted there was room for improvement or change was needed, representative comments included:

> [The need for] more training for strategic thinking and improving the quality of volunteers. Finding a way to enable good meetings to take place at a time staff and volunteers could make without being too onerous on either.

There are too many demands on governors' time: many requirements change quite quickly over time, and many are of secondary importance. There needs to be a clearer prioritisation of what governors should do so that they can concentrate on key strategic issues.

The changing policy landscape

Clearly to concentrate on key strategic issues and have confidence to manage a rapidly changing policy landscape schools requires confident and capable governing bodies and training and development will have a key role to play. The changing policy landscape and schools' responses to it was discussed in Chapter 2 when further analysis of headteacher responses enabled a typology of schools to be offered: the approach to policy developments was described as either confident, cautious, concerned or constrained. But what about chairs of governors, how did they view the changing policy landscape and did their views differ considerably from those of headteachers?

The 2012 survey showed that most chairs of governors (86%) like the headteachers (84%) felt their school had the confidence to manage current policy changes (see Table 5.8). Both groups of respondents were most positive about an increased focus on schools working together to promote improvements in pupil outcomes (with 85% of headteachers and 78% of chairs of governors thinking the impact would be positive or moderately positive).

Table 5.7 shows that although chairs of governors were positive about the Pupil Premium (48%), they were to a lesser extent than headteachers (66% felt this funding would impact positively or moderately positively on their school). Both groups of respondents were least positive about the changing role of local authorities, with 73 per cent of governors and 66 per cent of headteachers suggesting it would impact moderately negatively or negatively

TABLE 5.7 Views of the impact of government policy on schools, 2012

Policy and its impact on your school	Headteacher (*n* = 833)	Chair of governor (*n* = 347)
The potential for schools to become more independent and autonomous		
Positive/moderately positive	52	21
Negative/moderately negative	34	36
No impact	13	19
No response	1	24
The changing role of the LA		
Positive/moderately positive	27	15
Negative/moderately negative	66	72
No impact	5	7
No response	2	6
Fewer government-commissioned professional development programmes		
Positive/moderately positive	32	16
Negative/moderately negative	45	54
No impact	22	14
No response	1	17
The new Ofsted inspection framework		
Positive/moderately positive	36	43
Negative/moderately negative	43	19
No impact	20	19
No response	1	19
The Pupil Premium		
Positive/moderately positive	65	48
Negative/moderately negative	17	19
No impact	16	16
No response	2	16

Policy and its impact on your school	Headteacher (*n* = 833)	Chair of governor (*n* = 347)
Teaching Schools		
Positive/moderately positive	46	31
Negative/moderately negative	15	6
No impact	35	21
No response	4	42
An increased focus on schools working together to promote improvements in pupil outcomes		
Positive/moderately positive	85	78
Negative/moderately negative	3	2
No impact	11	12
No response	0	9
An expanding number of chains of schools		
Positive/moderately positive	30	25
Negative/moderately negative	31	15
No impact	33	23
No response	5	37
The increased number of national and local leaders of education (NLEs/LLEs)		
Positive/moderately positive	47	27
Negative/moderately negative	8	5
No impact	42	27
No response	3	41
The establishment of Free Schools		
Positive/moderately positive	3	4
Negative/moderately negative	54	30
No impact	35	40
No response	7	26
No response	3	19

Note: A series of single response items. The percentages in this table are weighted by school type, size and FSM. Due to rounding, percentages may not sum to 100.
Source: NFER and IoE leadership survey for the National College, 2012.

TABLE 5.8 Impact of policy on relationships with other schools

Are you encouraged or discouraged to . . .	Headteacher % (n = 833)	Chair of governor % (n = 347)
form collaborative partnerships with other schools		
Significantly encourage/encourage	65	59
Significantly discourage/discourage	4	6
Neither encourage or discourage	31	34
formally support another school's improvement		
Significantly encourage/encourage	50	45
Significantly discourage/discourage	7	7
Neither encourage or discourage	43	47
make decisions that will support the progress of other local schools		
Significantly encourage/encourage	43	34
Significantly discourage/discourage	8	7
Neither encourage or discourage	48	58
compete with other local schools for students and resources		
Significantly encourage/encourage	30	38
Significantly discourage/discourage	12	14
Neither encourage or discourage	57	48
undertake less partnership based activity and focus more on the needs of my own school		
Significantly encourage/encourage	23	22
Significantly discourage/discourage	27	23
Neither encourage or discourage	49	53

Note: A series of single response items. The percentages in this table are weighted by school type, size and FSM. Due to rounding, percentages may not sum to 100.
Source: NFER and IoE leadership survey for the National College, 2012. Earley et al., 2012.

on their schools. Less than one-half of headteachers (45%) and just over one-half of governors (54%), felt there would be a negative/moderately negative impact from fewer government-commissioned professional development programmes. Whereas just over one-half of headteachers (55%) were similarly negative about the establishment of Free Schools, this was the case for only 30 per cent of chairs.

Around two-fifths (43%) of headteachers thought the new Ofsted inspection framework would have a negative impact to some extent on their institution. Exactly the same percentage of governor responses saw the new framework in more positive terms.

The vast majority of chairs of governors (92%) thought that it was very important or quite important to work in partnership with other schools. Table 5.8 shows the impact of policy on relationships with other schools and the differences between the views of heads and chairs. The vast majority of headteachers (87%) and chairs of governors (83%) believed that working in partnership with other schools was critical to improving outcomes for students. Around 60 per cent of headteachers and governors felt that the current policy agenda encouraged their school to form collaborative partnerships with other schools. Exactly one-half of headteachers and 45 per cent of chairs felt that current policy encouraged them to formally support another school's improvement. Two-fifths (43%) of headteachers and a third (34%) of chairs of governors felt encouraged to make decisions that would support the progress of other schools. Headteachers were more neutral about the impact of policy on competition with other schools for students and resources. Two-fifths (41%) of headteachers strongly agreed/agreed that schools should be encouraged to sell advice and support services to other schools.

There was a general consensus between chairs of governors and headteachers about degrees of school autonomy. Approximately one-half of both groups agreed that greater autonomy would enable their schools to use financial resources to better support their own priorities and enable the school to improve teaching and learning. There was also general agreement that the school had plans about how it would use its greater autonomy. The vast majority of heads and chairs agreed that working in partnership with other schools was critical to improving outcomes for children. There were significant differences however between levels of agreement concerning schools selling advice and support services to other schools, with chairs (51%) keener on this than their heads (41%). Only one-fifth (19%) of chairs welcomed the opportunity for the school to become an academy. Heads were not asked directly about becoming an academy but just over one-half (52%) were positive about the potential to become more independent and autonomous. Only one-third of chairs of governors (34%) were attracted by the idea of the school joining a federation or chain of schools.

Summary

This chapter has examined the role of school governing bodies within the changing leadership landscape considering where governors are involved in leadership activities and how perceptions of their strategic leadership role have changed over the time of the baseline and leadership studies. Their training and development needs were also considered as were current views on the policy landscape. A key recommendation from the 2002 study was the need to enhance the overall strategic leadership role of governing bodies in schools and the findings from the various leadership research projects demonstrate that ten years on the strategic leadership role of the governing body is still an area that requires attention in some schools but for others it is a reality. It seems reasonable to say that governing body effectiveness, especially in operating strategically, has improved over the ten-year period covered by the studies. Support among both headteachers and governors for increasing the strategic leadership role of the governing body has increased, but ensuring that this happens in practice in all schools is the challenge that lies ahead. The Academies Commission (2013, p. 6) went as far as to suggest that there is a need for a radical shift in governing bodies' capacity, knowledge and attitude if they are to take on both the expected leadership role and fulfil their legal responsibilities as directors of charitable companies. Concerns continue to be raised about the capacity of volunteers to defend the school rigorously, challenge for improvement and be a critical friend, especially with a self-improving school-led system.

Providing training courses and offering development opportunities for governors are mechanisms to improve the effectiveness of the governing body and ensure they have a role as leaders. The 2007 study noted that governors wanted more training in order to better support school leaders of the future (PwC, 2007, p. 120) and with the new inspection framework focusing more explicitly on their role (Ofsted, 2012b), the demise of LA governor training provision and support may be a cause for concern.

6

The Balance Between Operational and Strategic Leadership

A key challenge to heads and other senior leaders in schools is achieving a balance across their various areas of responsibility and ensuring that they focus their time and attention on the things that matter most. Keeping their focus on strategic and learning-centred leadership is a continuing challenge. A recent report for the National College on *The Experiences of New Headteachers* (Earley et al., 2011) also echoed this state of affairs and noted how difficult new heads found it to get the balance right and ensure time was being spent on the 'right things'.

In this chapter the tasks of leaders and their use of time is considered. How has the situation changed since the first baseline leadership study in the early 2000s? How this time use compares with heads' ideal use, especially as it relates to strategic, entrepreneurial activities and leading teaching and learning, is also discussed drawing upon the findings of the 2012 landscape study. How school leaders work to improve teaching and learning is the key focus of the next chapter.

The tasks of leaders

The importance of school leaders, especially headteachers, and the key role they play in school success has been a common, recurring theme but what do school leaders actually do to bring about success? What does their daily work look like? For example, are the kind of activities they undertake helping their schools to improve or are they bogged down in form-filling and paperwork? The lists of leadership tasks are myriad and there are many lists of competences or standards required of school leaders (e.g. see Huber, 2004, 2010). More specifically, an Organisation for Economic and Cultural Development (OECD) report (Schleicher, 2012, p. 14) sees school leaders as helping to:

> define the school's educational goals, ensure that instructional practice is directed towards achieving these goals, observe and evaluate teachers, suggest modifications to improve teaching practices, shape their professional development, help solve problems that may arise within the classroom or among teachers and liaise with the community and parents. They are also in a position to provide incentives and motivate teachers to improve the quality of instruction.

Most national education systems have a document listing the roles and responsibilities of school leaders, usually expressed in terms of a personal specification and job responsibilities. The 2007 report used such a document for England, along with the National Standards for Headteachers (DfES, 2004), to divide headteachers' key activities into six areas of responsibility: strategic direction and ethos; managing teaching and learning; developing and managing people; networking and collaboration between schools and with other agencies; operational matters; and accountability (PwC, 2007, pp. 8–9). Their findings in relation to these areas are considered later in the chapter.

Other studies, especially those involving observation and shadowing as a research method, have drawn up more specific lists of tasks and activities usually divided into categories (e.g. leadership, management, administration, teaching, professional development, internal and external relations and personal) and subcategories (e.g. the broad category of 'teaching' might include not only teaching itself but conducting assemblies, clubs and trips with pupils). Research enquiring into headteacher activity often takes the form of self-reporting or responding to questionnaires which ask school leaders how they spend their time on various activities and which ones are given priority (e.g. Burkhauser et al., 2012; Earley, 2012; Earley and Bubb, 2013; Schleicher, 2012). As is shown later in the chapter, the 2007 and the 2012 leadership studies asked about use of time as part of their questionnaire surveys but unfortunately not in the same way or using a similar categorization of activities thus making direct comparison over time rather difficult.

Amount of time

An important source of information about headteachers' (and others') work that has drawn on a different form of self-report data collection is the diary-based studies from the School Teachers Review Body (STRB). The STRB studies provide information on how long school leaders and teachers work and the kind of activities they devote most of their time to. Heads and teachers in cooperating schools have completed diaries for a single week in early March from 1994 with annual surveys conducted since 2000. Figures 6.1 and 6.2, taken from one of their reports (Deakin et al., 2010) show the average total hours worked by headteachers, senior/middle leaders and teachers in primary and secondary schools over the decade, 2000–10. (Data for 2011–12 were not available at the time of writing.)

The charts show the hours worked on average by primary and secondary headteachers, deputy heads and classroom teachers from 2000 to 2010. The figures for 2010 were found to be significantly lower than in 2000, although for primary headteachers there had been an increase in average hours each year since 2005. The average total hours worked by primary heads has decreased from 58.9 hours per week in 2000 to 56.1 in 2010 (a difference of 2.8 hours), although since 2005 there has been a progressive increase. There has been a reduction in the total number of hours worked on average by deputy heads in primary schools from 56.2 hours per week in 2000 to 50.9 in 2010 (a difference of 5.3 hours).

The average number of hours worked by secondary school headteachers and deputy heads has been more changeable over time with fewer working hours per week on average in 2010 than in 2000. Secondary school heads reported working fewer hours in 2010 per week (57.3) than in 2000 (60.8) (a difference of 3.5 hours). The average total hours worked by deputy heads

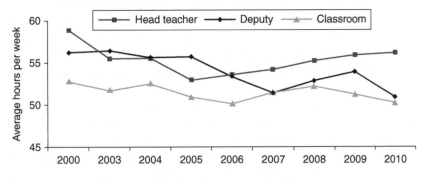

FIGURE 6.1 *Average total hours – primary schools 2000–10.*

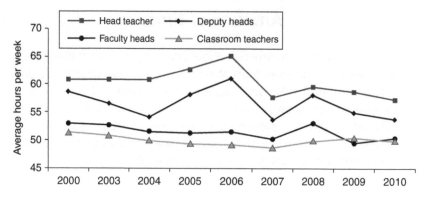

FIGURE 6.2 *Average total hours – secondary schools 2000–10.*

in secondary schools has fallen from 58.6 hours per week in 2000 to 53.7 in 2010 (a difference of 4.9 hours) and a decreasing trend since 2008. In 2000 heads of faculty/department in secondary schools worked 52.9 hours per week, on average; this has decreased to 50.3 in 2010 (a difference of 2.6 hours).

The STRB data also show that school leaders, regardless of phase, work at least a fifth of their weekly working hours (around 10 hours) outside what might be regarded as their normal working day. The number of hours primary and secondary senior leaders spent teaching has fallen over the decade. For example from 6 to 4.7 hours for primary headteachers and from 3.4 hours to just 1.2 hours for their secondary colleagues.

Those completing their workload diaries in 2010 were also asked a series of attitudinal questions. Two-thirds of secondary headteachers (67%) reported having the time to do their job as it should be done most or all the time. Interestingly, this figure had risen from 40 per cent in 2008. However, less than half (46%) of primary headteachers reported having the time to do the job as it should be done. Secondary deputy heads reported the opposite view to their heads, with fewer indicating that they had the time to do the job as it should be done in 2010 (38%) compared to 2008 (44%). This was also the case for deputy heads in primary schools with just over a third (37%) compared to over two-thirds (68%) in 2008 reporting that they had the time to do their job.

These variations in hours worked over time, phase of school and leadership position cannot easily be explained although the government's remodelling agenda and school workforce reforms, beginning in the mid-2000s, were attempts to reduce teachers' working hours and introduce a better work-life balance (Bubb and Earley, 2004). As a result of these initiatives, the number of support staff, including school business managers or bursars, employed in schools has risen significantly and although teachers' working hours per week declined this appeared to be to the detriment of school leaders' workloads, especially headteachers (Hutchings et al., 2009; Ofsted, 2010b).

Use of time

Over the last decade, the STRB studies provide longitudinal information on how long school leaders work and the kind of activities (e.g. teaching, planning, preparation and assessment, school/staff management, administrative support, individual/professional activity) they devote time to. The baseline and leadership studies did not always ask heads specific questions about their use of time across various matters although broad questions were asked about use of time and prioritization. The 2002 baseline and 2005 leadership studies asked heads about the activities they undertook in the classroom and while in the early 2000s 'the majority of heads were still very much involved in the teaching and learning which goes on in their schools' (Earley et al., 2002, p. 35) this had changed a little by the time of the next study in 2005. Stevens et al.'s (2005, p. 32) findings suggest that headteachers' activities in the classroom had altered and they were spending less time teaching regular timetabled lessons. Just over half (55%) said they undertook regular timetabled teaching commitments compared with nearly two-thirds (62%) of headteachers in 2002. Indeed, when asked directly, a third of headteachers (35%) said they spent less time in the classroom compared with three years ago, while a fifth said the time had decreased 'a lot'. Only a fifth of headteachers (19%) said they spent more time in the classroom and a quarter (27%) said their time in the classroom had remained the same. Almost three-quarters (73%) of headteachers covered for absent colleagues compared with 65% in 2002, and 11 per cent covered for unfilled vacancies (8% in 2002). Among these tasks, most headteachers were also involved in monitoring and evaluation (95%) and 42 per cent said they undertook administrative tasks in the classroom. Monitoring and evaluation and administrative tasks were not included in the 2002 study although 85 per cent of the headteachers in the 2002 study reported that 'observation' was undertaken. However, the biggest change recorded between the two studies was that headteachers were spending more time coaching their colleagues than in 2002 (54% compared with 30%).

The 2005 study also found, perhaps surprisingly, that secondary school headteachers were more likely than primaries to cover for absent colleagues (79% and 69%, respectively), have regular teaching commitments (62% and 49%) and cover for unfilled vacancies (14% and 7%). However, primary school headteachers were more likely than their secondary colleagues to undertake administrative tasks (45% and 36%, respectively) (Stevens et al., 2005, pp. 32–3).

The 2007 research did not collect data from heads in a similar format to the earlier studies but did ask heads which activities (from a list of 18 items) took up most of their time over the school year. The top five activities were reported to be: accountability (81%), responsibility for pupils' well-being (60%), school improvement planning (57%), implementing new ideas/initiatives (57%) and management of teachers (48%). The heads were also asked which three, in their view, should be their most important activities as a headteacher over the school year. The following activities were recorded as priorities: strategic vision (58%), school improvement planning (49%), responsibility for pupils' well-being (46%) and accountability (44%) also being frequently noted. Strategic vision had earlier been recorded as the eighth highest ranking activity for taking up time over the year (30%).

The 2007 report noted that school leaders work, in general, long hours and have difficulty in achieving an appropriate work-life balance. The STRB data discussed above generally supports this picture of a long working week linked to the increasing number and complexity of tasks for which heads are responsible.

The 2007 report draws upon both its quantitative and qualitative data findings to offer the following comments about school leaders' use of time and activity concerning the six responsibilities mentioned earlier: strategic direction and ethos; managing teaching and learning; developing and managing people; networking and collaboration between schools and with other agencies; operational matters; and accountability (PwC, 2007, pp. vi–vii).

- Strategic direction and ethos

'Many headteachers recognise themselves that they are struggling to create sufficient time to engage effectively in the various strategic issues they are required to deal with' (p. vi). The sheer volume of operational delivery issues that school leaders had to address were responsible for this in part. PwC suggest that some school leaders were 'more comfortable with an operational role rather than a strategic one' (p. vi).

- Teaching and learning

'There is a widespread recognition across the sector that an essential role of school leaders is to promote and develop the quality of teaching and learning delivered in the school' (p. vi). The PwC report notes that frustration was expressed that the current environment does not allow school leaders to be as involved in this area as they would like. It is noted that 'in order to enable them to devote sufficient time to leadership and management, school leaders themselves teach a lot less than they used to; for example, just over one quarter of primary and secondary heads do not teach at all in timetabled lessons, and most of the rest teach for less than five hours per week' (p. vi).

- Developing and managing people

'Developing people and nurturing talent is a key strategic leadership issue facing all types of organisations across different sectors. Within the schools context, the international literature shows that one of the most important ways in which school leaders contribute to teaching and learning is through their impact on the motivation, development and well-being of staff' (p. vi). Evidence from the 2007 research study demonstrates that 'many school leaders have embraced these challenges in relation to people development well, but also that there is more to be done, at both institution and system level . . . and many school leaders may not have embraced the people agenda as fully as has been the case in other sectors (e.g. in the private sector where it is one of the bedrocks on which all current thinking on leadership is based)' (p. vi).

- Networking and collaboration

The 2007 report notes that the policy imperatives of multi-agency working, collaboration and school networking will become the rule and not the exception and 'this raises the need for school leaders . . . to collaborate effectively with other agencies to secure the delivery of these services . . . More generally, all of this means that school leaders now have to be much more outward looking than they used to be, and this has clear implications around the need for a range of 'softer' interpersonal skills relating to networking and communication' (p. vi). The PwC report notes that most school leaders acknowledge the new requirements being placed on them in these areas, 'but that many are struggling to respond, and most recognise the need for training and support' (p. vi).

- Operations

Many school leaders were found to be 'too involved in operational and delivery matters and that this has been, to some extent, at the expense of embracing their more strategic imperatives' (p. vii). Stories of headteachers unblocking toilets, filling dishwashers and supervizing pupils before and after school were noted. 'Sometimes such behaviours can be appropriate, and they are often driven by resources, particularly in the primary sector, where the opportunities for delegating such tasks can be limited. But these ties to the operational space also seem to be related, based on our interpretation of the evidence, to a mindset amongst some school leaders which is more comfortable with an operational than a strategic role' (p. vii).

● Accountability

Accountability was found to be the most time-consuming of all the activities carried out by headteachers. 'In this context, the word "initiativitis" was often used by the leaders we spoke to as a way of expressing their frustration with the number of policy initiatives they were having to deal with, the apparent inconsistencies between them and the lack of resources to deal with them' (p. vii). The 2007 report noted

> a wish for a stability and consistency which cannot be delivered and which is not enjoyed by any other organisation in the public or private sector. We know from other sectors that change, diversity and complexity are inevitable features of the current and future environment and that leaders need to accept and embrace this. School leaders can, however, legitimately expect such change to be managed coherently and in a joined-up manner by Government and other agencies. (2007, p. vii)

For the 2007 report the new policy contexts in which school headteachers were operating were very likely to have an effect on their roles and responsibilities and that of the wider leadership team. For example, the leadership team would increasingly include financial or business managers and professionals such as 'cluster managers', dependent on the needs of the school. These new contexts were seen as having implications for the school leader role, particularly in terms of relationship-building, performance management and accountability, as they became increasingly involved with, or responsible for, multi-agency teams. The policy changes made between the time of the 2007 study (mid-2000s) and the most recent leadership landscape study (early 2010s) has meant that only some of the implications have been realized (e.g. the demise of the every child matters [ECM] and multi-agency agendas and the growth of academisation and chains).

The 2007 research asked leaders to comment on how they saw their role changing or developing over the next five years (i.e. up to 2012). The majority of leaders believed that their role would become more strategic in nature and the term 'system leadership' was used to describe how there would be greater collaboration and cooperation between schools. 'Leaders from better performing schools would be increasingly encouraged to help and assist leaders in less well performing schools' (PwC, 2007, p. x). Mixed views were offered in 2007 regarding the idea of schools being run and managed like a business, with headteachers taking greater responsibility for strategic issues, and thus having less day-to-day contact with staff and/or pupils. Some respondents viewed this scenario more positively than having to juggle teaching with administration. Others favoured shifting some administrative tasks to non-teaching leaders (e.g. school business managers) in order to allow more time to concentrate on teaching and learning.

The 2012 study

The 2012 leadership landscape study also explored the theme of leadership tasks and senior leaders' use of time. Headteachers were asked to estimate the percentage of time they spent in each of three locations – in the office, inside the school (but outside the office) and outside the office on official school business – during a typical working week. Results from the 2012 headteacher survey show, on average, heads spend most of their time in their office (51%), followed by time inside school outside of their office (14%). Although, on average, the least amount of time was spent outside school, this ranged from zero to 60 per cent of a headteacher's time. This recorded time allocation is remarkably similar to that reported by McKinsey (Barber et al., 2010) which found that English heads spent 14 per cent of their time outside school on official business, 34 per cent in school but outside the office and over half of their time (52%) in their office.

In the 2012 survey, both headteachers and senior/middle leaders, were also asked how much time they spent on various activities in comparison to how much time they would like to spend. The seven categories were not specifically defined and are shown in Table 6.1. The table compares heads' and senior/middle leaders' time spent on tasks. It shows that over a half of respondents (62% of heads and 53% of senior leaders) felt they spent the 'right amount' of time on leadership generally. Further analysis found that this response was more likely from heads of 'outstanding' schools. However, around a third of both heads and senior/middle leaders considered that 'too little time' was spent on leadership generally compared with how much time they would like to spend.

Heads (58%) and other senior leaders (49%) considered that 'too little time' was spent on the leadership of teaching and learning, although about four out of ten thought it 'about right'. There were no significant differences between primary and secondary respondents in relation to leading teaching and learning. Leadership of teaching and learning or learning-centred leadership is the focus of the next chapter.

Over one-half (55%) of both groups said management time was 'about right', while further analysis showed secondary school heads and academy senior/middle leaders were more likely than others to say this. Leaders of academies were least likely to say that 'too much' time was spent on management, while heads from low Free School Meals (FSM) schools and senior/middle leaders from primary schools were more likely to say that 'too little time' was spent on management. Notable proportions of heads and senior leaders (38% and 23%) also said they spent 'too much time' on management.

Heads and other school leaders were most likely to say that they spent too much time on administration (69% of headteachers and 70% of senior/middle leaders), with senior/middle leaders in state maintained schools more likely to respond in this way.

Table 6.1 also shows that a notable proportion of leaders felt they spent 'too little time' on their own teaching and professional development. Further analysis showed that senior/middle leaders from secondary and 'satisfactory/ inadequate' Ofsted graded schools were more likely to respond in this way. More leaders of secondary schools and academies were likely to respond that time given to their own teaching was 'about right'.

The 2012 survey also asked heads whether over the last 18 months there had been any change in the time they had spent on entrepreneurial activities, which were defined as seeking out new opportunities and resources, developing new partnerships and networking to promote the school's interests. In the last 18 months, the amount of time spent on entrepreneurial activities had broadly stayed the same for 47 per cent of headteachers and increased for 42 per cent of them. For one-in-ten it had decreased. There were no statistically significant differences by phase of school.

Balancing strategic and operational demands on leadership time has been a constant challenge and Table 6.2 shows the ways headteachers try to cope. Most headteachers (89%) encouraged and enabled other teachers to contribute to school leadership, and had been doing so either in the last year or for a year or more. Just over three-quarters of headteachers (78%) had delegated or further embedded more strategic responsibilities across the senior team. Most heads reported widening senior leadership team (SLT) membership but 40 per cent had no current plans to do so. Secondary schools were more likely to widen SLT membership than primary schools. Most headteachers (88%) said there were no plans to develop an executive head or head of school model to help balance demands on time.

One-half of heads (49%) reported having appointed a school business manager or bursar for a year or more. Secondary schools were more likely to say that they had been trying to develop the school business manager post into a senior team role.

The 2012 research included interviews with 20 headteachers that explored further the relationship between the operational and the strategic. The phrase used by one of the interviewees, 'the important but non-urgent', captures those aspects of the leadership role for which there was insufficient time.

TABLE 6.1 Time spent on tasks (%) – heads and senior/middle leaders

	Heads	Senior leaders
Leadership generally		
Too little time	32	37
About right	62	53
Too much time	6	10
Leadership of teaching and learning specifically		
Too little time	58	49
About right	40	42
Too much time	1	6
Management		
Too little time	6	20
About right	55	56
Too much time	38	23
Administration		
Too little time	2	7
About right	28	21
Too much time	69	70
Your own teaching		
Too little time	47	34
About right	43	50
Too much time	6	12
Leading beyond the school/partnership work		
Too little time	27	42
About right	66	51
Too much time	4	5
Own professional development		
Too little time	57	46
About right	42	51
Too much time	1	2
Non response = 1% Total	833	769

Source: Earley et al., 2012, p. 82.

TABLE 6.2 Strategies to help balance strategic and operational demands

Balancing strategic and operational demands				
Please indicate which strategies, if any, you have used to date to help balance strategic and operational demands on leadership time (%)	We have been doing this for a year or more (%)	Yes we have done this in the last 12 months (%)	Plan to do so in the next 12 months (%)	No current plans to do so (%)	No response (%)
Appointed school business manager or bursar	49	10	9	30	1
Developed school business manager/ bursar post into a senior team role	30	10	16	43	2
Delegated or further embedded more strategic responsibilities across senior team	38	40	11	9	1
Widened SLT membership	23	22	12	40	2
Built a flatter less hierarchical leadership structure and ethos	38	23	8	28	3
Encouraged and enabled teachers to contribute to school leadership	52	37	9	1	1
Shared specific leadership responsibilities with a partner or across a family of schools	14	14	16	55	1
Developed an executive head and head of school model	5	1	3	88	2

Note: N = 833. A series of single response items. The percentages in this table are weighted by school type and FSM. Due to rounding, percentages may not sum to 100.
Source: Earley et al., 2012, p. 84.

'Supporting staff, developing the teaching and learning', 'being in the classroom', 'finding ways to be creative with the curriculum and overcome barriers to learning' were tasks that headteachers believed were fundamental in their work and on which they could never spend too much time. Modelling the behaviours and expectations they have of their staff team were important, especially when working with pupils with challenging and diverse needs: 'I never ask anyone to do anything that I do not show I will do myself'.

Finding time for strategic planning, both individually and with senior teams was difficult for many headteachers. Several spoke of ways in which they planned ahead to make time, such as having awaydays and weekends with the senior team, ensuring that strategic issues were discussed at regular leadership meetings and even using 'driving time' for thinking issues through. Research, keeping up to date with teaching and learning innovations and time for thorough evaluation were also squeezed into time that was never felt to be sufficient.

Partnership working was considered important for school development but some noted how it was reducing opportunities to be a 'visible' head, present on corridors and in playgrounds for pupils and parents. Although recognizing that others in the school were competent in leading the school in their absence, it was still considered a 'balancing act' on how much time to spend in working with and supporting other schools and partnerships as well as keeping focus on maintaining success in one's own institution. This was a challenge that needed to be resolved before one could engage in 'system leadership' work (Earley and Weindling, 2006).

The demands of administration and bureaucracy had not diminished and comments were made, as in the earlier 2007 study, on the particular pressure of increasing accountability. 'Too much time' was being spent keeping up to date with changes and reconciling these with the core priorities of the school. Changes arising from increasing school autonomy and moving to academy status were, reported as time-consuming but necessary. Reacting to urgent operational issues took up much time and although this was recognized as essential it significantly reduced the time needed for other important areas of work and made inroads into heads' personal time and work-life balance.

The time-consuming issues mentioned most frequently were those related to staff, parent and pupil issues. Child protection cases, serious pupil discipline issues, community issues, staff redundancies and disciplinaries, and the need to be available to help staff work through personal issues affecting their work, build confidence or smooth relationships were mentioned by nearly all of the 20 heads interviewed. Some mentioned the impact of the downturn in the economy on the local community and a rise in parent issues as significant consumers of their time. Managing cuts in budgets and finance was taking up time, despite good support provided by school business managers (Earley et al., 2012, pp. 82–4).

Case study: Balance between operational and strategic

An outstanding primary school which gained academy status in September 2011 was amongst the first tranche of primary schools in England to adopt academy status. The headteacher was extremely experienced with over 25 years teaching.

Children entered the school with average levels of attainment and left with attainment levels in excess of national averages. This robust level of progress was maintained through strong leadership and focus on children's learning. The growth of teaching assistants in supporting teaching and learning had also contributed greatly to the success of the school. Governance at the school was stable, effective and knowledgeable, drawing in a range of governors with knowledge and experience in financial management and handling performance data.

For the headteacher in particular, in the conversion to academy status, more time had been spent in entrepreneurial activities in terms of developing relationships with potential partners and clients for school improvement services that the school is planning to grow. More time spent on teaching activity and leading teaching and learning was regarded as rewarding and the core function of educators and leaders. However, balancing this with a strategic role of headship was recognized as an inherent challenge. A shared leadership approach, with responsibility and accountability residing across SLT and middle leaders with a fundamental contribution from governors in terms of ongoing monitoring and challenge, was being developed.

Source: Earley et al., 2012, p. 90.

Summary

All of the studies into school leader activity consistently show that the work of heads is fast paced, stressful, relentless, fragmented, involving a wide variety and range of activities ('no such thing as a typical day') and responsive to the needs of others in the school (Earley, 2012; Earley and Bubb, 2013). Data derived from observation, shadowing, self-report studies and weekly logs show a consistent picture of a high volume, relentless, complex and emotionally demanding workload (e.g. Bristow et al., 2007; MacBeath et al., 2009). The research shows heads spend much of their time dealing with the administrative and managerial aspects of the job. They like to be highly visible and 'walk the talk'. However, both the 2012 study and the McKinsey report (Barber et al., 2010) note that English heads spent about 14 per cent of their time outside school on official business, 35 per cent in school but outside the office and over half of their time (52%) in the head's office.

In the 2012 research, heads considered it a 'balancing act' on how much time to spend in working with and supporting other schools and partnerships as well as keeping focus on maintaining success in one's own institution. The majority of school leaders felt they spent the right amount of time on leadership but that they spent too much time on administration and management. Not enough time was spent on the leadership of teaching and learning and on their own teaching and professional development. To help balance strategic and operational demands on leadership time, almost all headteachers encouraged and enabled other teachers to contribute to school leadership. Just over three-quarters delegated or further embedded more strategic responsibilities across the SLT. Many schools, especially in the secondary sector, appointed school business managers or bursars, to help enable a greater focus on teaching and learning. It is this focus that is the subject of the next chapter.

7

How School Leaders Work to Improve Teaching and Learning

Over the ten-year period considered in this book, the notion of learning-centred leadership or leadership for learning (Hallinger, 2012) has continued to gain primacy over other conceptions of leadership: how leaders undertake such leadership is the subject of this chapter. It draws upon various data sets to address questions about the nature of learning-centred leadership and its enactment in England and other countries. A theory of learning-centred leadership is outlined and, drawing on the 2012 landscape study, the most important actions being taken by school leaders to lead the improvement of teaching and learning are explored. Research is drawn upon to illuminate how school leaders operate in schools and classrooms to enhance the quality of teaching and learning. In conclusion, case studies of headteachers show how leaders attempt to work in a learning-centred manner.

Involvement in educational matters

For the Organisation for Economic and Cultural Development's (OECD's) comparative review of school leadership – *Improving School Leadership* – the core of effective leadership was to focus on supporting, evaluating and developing teacher quality (Pont et al., 2008). As noted in a more recent OECD report, this included 'coordinating the curriculum and teaching program, monitoring and evaluating teaching practice, promoting teachers' professional development, and supporting collaborative work cultures' (Schleicher, 2012, p. 18). In Sweden, for example, school leaders devote time to giving feedback to teachers:

> They also tend to frequently challenge the assumptions of their staff. By asking questions such as 'How do we know that?', 'Could we test another

way of doing it?' and 'What do we know about how people in other schools do it?' they help to foster a learning atmosphere in the school. (ibid., p. 18)

The OECD report (Schleicher, 2012) draws upon 2009 PISA data to consider school principals' views on their involvement in school matters across 34 member countries. The data, shown in Figure 7.1, are fascinating and demonstrate how education systems and their leaders attend to various school matters and how 'learning atmospheres' may differ. The 14 activities listed in the figure might broadly be defined as constituting learning-centred leadership as each one is concerned with an aspect of teaching and learning. Among OECD countries, for example, 61 per cent of students attend schools whose leaders 'quite often' or 'very often' take exam results into account when making decisions regarding curriculum development; two-thirds of students attend schools whose leaders 'quite often' or 'very often' monitor students' work; and 29 per cent attend schools whose leaders 'quite often' or 'very often' take over lessons from teachers who are unexpectedly absent. Clear differences can be seen in the enactment of the headteacher role between member countries. For example, the 50 per cent average for principal involvement in classroom observation was much higher in the United Kingdom (93%) and the United States (95%). The principal's role was more homogeneous across schools in Denmark and Norway while the variation in role was found to be greatest in Chile, Korea and the United States (see Figure 7.1).

The OECD report notes that studies in some member countries have shown how school leaders are affected by the growing demands on their time. The 2007 leadership research showed nearly two-thirds (61%) of headteachers in England described their work-life balance as poor or very poor, due 'to long working hours or to deficiencies in working practices, such as school heads not knowing how to prioritise or delegate their work' (Schleicher, 2012, p. 18). Administrative demands took up about one-third of headteachers' time, competing with educational leadership as their top priority. In New Zealand, Wylie (2007) found that, eight years after major education reforms were introduced, school leaders' administrative work had increased substantially and they were working ten hours longer per week, on average, than before the reforms. As was shown in the previous chapter, this was not the case for England where the number of hours worked had gradually declined over the last ten years (Deakin et al., 2010). Indeed, the OECD goes as far as to say that the UK (reference is to the UK and not England) is 'doing what school principals should be doing – spending time focused on learning, not administration' (Schleicher, 2012, p. 18). Headteachers' roles and their use of time show many similarities but clearly there are important variations both between and within education systems.

School principals' views of their involvement in school matters
Index of school principal's leadership based on school principals' reports

A	I make sure that the professional development activities of teachers are in accordance with the teaching goals of the school.
B	I ensure that teachers work according to the school's educational goals.
C	I observe instruction in classrooms.
D	I use student performance results to develop the school's educational goals.
E	I give teachers suggestions as to how they can improve their teaching.
F	I monitor students' work.
G	When a teacher has problems in his/her classroom, I take the initiative to discuss matters.
H	I inform teachers about possibilities for updating their knowledge and skills.
I	I check to see whether classroom activities are in keeping with our educational goals.
J	I take exam results into account in decisions regarding curriculum development.
K	I ensure that there is clarity concerning the responsibility for co-ordinating the curriculum.
L	When a teacher brings up a classroom problem, we solve the problem together.
M	I pay attention to disruptive behaviour in classrooms.
N	I take over lessons from teachers who are unexpectedly absent.

Percentage of students in schools whose principals reported that the following activities and behaviours occurred "quite often" or "very often" during the last school year

Range between top and bottom quarter — Average index — Variability in the index (Standard Deviation)

	A	B	C	D	E	F	G	H	I	J	K	L	M	N	Variability
Australia	98	99	64	93	76	58	89	95	81	81	97	93	94	32	1.0
Austria	89	92	41	60	67	86	84	79	67	22	75	92	87	53	0.8
Belgium	95	97	43	42	68	33	89	90	82	46	74	98	96	4	0.8
Canada	98	98	77	91	86	60	95	95	86	63	87	99	98	19	1.0
Chile	97	98	55	93	95	73	90	96	82	84	94	97	97	62	1.1
Czech Republic	95	98	57	81	79	93	86	98	83	59	93	96	75	23	0.8
Denmark	86	89	25	44	53	39	94	91	76	25	76	99	95	29	0.6
Estonia	92	94	59	84	58	75	72	93	57	62	87	83	79	24	0.9
Finland	64	75	9	46	40	61	77	95	59	13	77	98	94	39	0.7
France	w	w	w	w	w	w	w	w	w	w	w	w	w	w	w
Germany	82	94	40	57	53	82	80	85	57	33	73	95	84	42	0.7
Greece	40	78	12	61	53	46	97	96	67	34	69	98	96	63	1.0
Hungary	93	99	54	84	62	84	89	91	65	73	86	94	91	41	0.8
Iceland	88	89	39	78	77	69	87	96	54	58	87	100	75	26	0.7
Ireland	88	88	14	64	41	50	88	92	62	78	88	97	97	39	0.9
Israel	94	99	46	87	85	81	94	89	86	90	94	97	98	26	0.9
Italy	97	99	39	86	75	87	96	98	88	77	92	98	98	18	0.9
Japan	43	51	37	30	38	40	29	50	31	37	29	61	60	17	0.9
Korea	80	85	42	64	68	56	75	69	60	46	63	79	68	7	1.2
Luxembourg	87	98	32	65	52	64	96	67	74	32	47	98	98	23	1.0
Mexico	95	97	68	94	89	90	95	91	92	62	90	97	96	43	1.0
Netherlands	95	97	52	66	73	50	76	82	79	75	80	86	71	16	0.7
New Zealand	99	98	68	98	73	42	78	84	74	87	97	83	94	12	1.0
Norway	81	88	24	70	79	55	90	91	48	47	81	98	95	28	0.6
Poland	94	97	93	95	89	96	91	99	92	71	80	97	93	37	0.8
Portugal	93	97	9	94	65	49	91	89	48	82	97	99	97	7	0.7
Slovak Republic	97	99	86	87	86	90	86	98	91	76	96	91	91	15	0.7
Slovenia	99	100	77	78	85	90	90	95	85	65	93	98	94	23	0.8
Spain	86	97	28	85	55	45	86	86	66	71	92	99	99	63	0.9
Sweden	90	96	38	83	63	29	89	90	52	68	93	98	87	13	0.8
Switzerland	72	82	64	34	60	61	85	80	59	17	54	92	83	31	0.8
Turkey	85	95	70	93	85	90	75	90	87	78	93	97	99	36	0.9
United Kingdom	100	100	93	100	92	88	90	96	95	97	99	96	97	29	0.9
United States	98	98	95	96	94	72	95	97	94	88	90	97	96	16	1.1
OECD average	88	93	50	75	69	66	86	89	72	61	82	94	90	29	0.9

FIGURE 7.1 *Heads' views on involvement in school matters (Schleicher, 2012, p. 17).*

The evidence that leadership makes a difference to teaching and learning is strong. For example, the annual report of Ofsted notes that:

The quality of leadership and management makes a critical contribution to the quality of teaching and learning. The same (inspection) judgements for the quality of leadership and the quality of teaching were made in 80% of schools inspected this year. (Ofsted, 2012a, p. x)

The link between leadership and learning is becoming clearer. We know from international research studies that school leaders improve teaching and learning indirectly and most powerfully through their influence on staff motivation, commitment and working conditions (Day et al., 2009, 2011; Hallinger and Heck, 2010). The effect of school leaders is largely *indirect*; what leaders do and say, how they demonstrate leadership, does affect pupil learning outcomes but it is largely through the actions of others, most obviously teachers, that the effects of school leadership are mediated. Achieving results through others is the essence of leadership and it is the 'avenues of leader influence' that matter most (Hallinger and Heck, 2003, pp. 220–6). The impact or effects of leaders can be *direct* – where leaders' actions directly influence school outcomes – or *indirect* – where leaders affect outcomes indirectly through other variables. *Reciprocal* effects occur when leaders affect teachers and teachers affect the leaders and through these processes outcomes are affected (Southworth, 2004).

A report by McKinsey (Barber et al., 2010) notes that there is clear evidence in the international literature that developing teachers makes the biggest contribution to student learning outcomes and that the actions of school leaders are crucial for creating that 'learning atmosphere' for both pupils and staff. This finding is derived largely from the work of Robinson and her colleagues in New Zealand (Robinson et al., 2009; Robinson, 2011) who conducted a meta-analysis of 23 international studies to derive the key factors associated with effective school leadership. They used statistical data to establish effect sizes (ES) for five dimensions of leadership in terms of impact on student learning. Effect sizes are measured on a scale of zero to one where anything below 0.2 shows a weak or no effect, and anything greater than 0.6 reveals a significant impact. Their results were striking, with leadership related to teacher development having by far the greatest impact on students. The five dimensions and effect sizes were:

1 Promoting and participating in teacher learning and development (ES 0.84)

2 Planning, coordinating and evaluating teaching and the curriculum (ES 0.42)

3   Establishing goals and expectations (ES 0.35)

4   Strategic resourcing (ES 0.34)

5   Ensuring an orderly and supportive environment (ES 0.27)

The central message emerging from the meta-analysis was clear: 'The more leaders focus their relationships, their work and their learning on the core business of teaching and learning the greater their influence on student outcomes' (Robinson et al., 2009, p. 201). Learning-centred leadership is vital yet as noted in the previous chapter nearly six-out-of-ten heads claimed they spent 'too little time' on the leadership of teaching and learning and only about four-out-of-ten thought it was 'about right' (see Table 6.1).

Learning-centred leadership

Learning-centred leadership or what the Americans tend to call instructional or pedagogic leadership sees the principal or headteacher as 'lead learner' and learning, the core business of educational organizations, is paramount but conceptualized at a number of levels – pupil, adult and organizational learning (Swaffield and MacBeath, 2008). It is about focusing on teaching and learning but as shown in the previous chapter this can be one of many pressures and competing priorities on school leaders' time. For Levin, writing about 'confident leadership', the knowledge base about leading teaching and learning tells school leaders that:

> to do this work well, they have to: identify the work of leading learning as a key responsibility, to which they devote a considerable amount of time and attention and which takes priority over other competing pressures. (Levin, 2013, pp. 5–6)

The notion of instructional leadership was discussed in the 2002 baseline study. Two prescriptive models of leadership were said to have pre-eminent status within the field at that time – transformational and instructional or pedagogic leadership. The latter model assumed that the main focus for school leaders should be the actions of staff as they 'engage in activities directly affecting the quality of teaching and learning in the pursuit of enhanced pupil outcomes' (Earley et al., 2002, p. 81). In 2002 there were many organizational matters that school leaders could work at to enable improved learning to take place in classrooms. For example, they could:

● control better particular constraints on the amount of time pupils spend on particular tasks;

- differently legislate for the number of pupils in particular classrooms and their mix of gender, ethnicity, or ages;

- influence the working patterns of teachers by rearranging physical space and 'free' time to promote new norms of collegiality and experimentation;

- use discretionary resources (money, release time, etc.) to encourage and enhance innovative instructional activity;

- foster agreement about the appropriate level of teacher-expectation needed to encourage higher levels of pupil motivation;

- facilitate debate about what counts as a 'good lesson', what theories of learning are appropriate to the achievement of particular curricular objectives, and the form feedback received by pupils should take on what is acceptable performance in school. (p. 81)

The term learning-centred leadership was brought to the fore in England in the mid-2000s through the work of Geoff Southworth when he was director of research at the National College. For Southworth (2004, 2009, 2011) learning-centred leadership operates in three main ways through modelling, monitoring and dialogue. West-Burnham and Coates (2005) later added mentoring and coaching to these ways of working. Such leaders are concerned to promote and develop their institutions as learning-centred organizations or professional learning communities (Stoll and Seashore Louis, 2007; Stoll, 2011) in order to help bring about the school's objectives (Bubb and Earley, 2010). What do these terms mean and how do leaders operate as learning-centred leaders?

It was noted above that school leaders influence what happens in classrooms mainly in an indirect way – where leaders affect student outcomes indirectly through other variables – or as Southworth notes 'effective school leaders work directly on their indirect influence' (2004, p. 102). They do this through the careful deployment of school structures and systems, and deploy the related strategies of modelling, monitoring, dialogue (not monologue!) including mentoring and coaching. Southworth discusses in detail the first three strategies and processes and a brief account is offered below.

Modelling is about the power of example. Teachers and leaders are strong believers in setting an example because they know this influences students and colleagues alike. 'Teachers watch what leaders do in order to check whether the leaders' actions are consistent over time and to test whether their leaders do as they say. Teachers do not follow leaders who cannot 'walk the talk' (Southworth, 2009, p. 95).

Monitoring includes the careful analysis of students' progress and outcome data (e.g. assessment and test scores, evaluation data, performance trends, parental opinion surveys, student attendance data, student interview information) and then acting upon these data. The amount of information available about student and school performance in England has grown apace over the last decade and can be used for a variety of purposes including self-evaluation. Since the late 2010s a huge amount of data about every school is publicly available from the Department for Education (DfE) website (www.education. dfe.gov), while in 2013 Ofsted, the inspection agency for England, issued what it called 'data dashboards' which can be used by parents and school governors to gain an informed picture of a school's performance. Schools, including their governing bodies, have since the early 2000s had access to more detailed performance reports in the form of (password protected) PANDAs (performance and assessment reports) and, more recently, RAISEonline reports (reporting and analysis for improvement through self-evaluation).

Undertaking monitoring also involves school leaders visiting classrooms, observing teachers at work and providing them with feedback. Although the intention is to make this process educative and developmental for both parties some of this will be judgemental and is a valuable part of performance management. In addition Ofsted expects school leaders to know the quality of its teachers and may ask to be informed of the school's best and worst performers. Southworth notes that monitoring enables leaders 'not only to keep in touch with colleagues' classrooms, but also to develop, over time, knowledge of teachers' strengths and development needs. It is a diagnostic assessment of colleagues' skills, strengths and craft knowledge' (ibid., p. 97). The latter is a critical feature of learning-centred organizations and professional learning communities.

Southworth's third strategy or way of working for learning-centred leaders – dialogue – is about creating opportunities for teachers to talk with their colleagues and leaders about learning and teaching. 'Both classrooms and staffrooms are places where there is a lot of talk. Indeed, there is no shortage of talk in schools. Yet, there is sometimes too little conversation about teaching and learning' (ibid., p. 97). He makes the important point that we all learn from experience, but not as much as we might and

> without leaders to facilitate our learning we sometimes learn very little from our work. Dialogues with teachers include encouragement, feedback and questioning about teaching. It is more powerful when based on classroom observation. (ibid., p. 97)

West-Burnham and Coates (2005) added mentoring and coaching to Sothworth's three strategies as they saw it as underpinning everything within a school community. There are many different definitions of these terms, for example, mentoring is usually seen as being guided and offered advice by a more experienced colleague, whereas coaching is a way of moving another person's thinking forward – a form of empowerment. The process helps individuals gain confidence, believe in themselves and find answers from within. Coaching is a process, a methodology that can be used to assist colleagues through a problem or issue they have.

For Southworth learning-centred leadership is about:

> the simultaneous use of these strategies in ways which mutually reinforce one another. It is their combined effect which creates powerful learning for teachers and leaders and which, in turn, inform teachers' actions in classrooms and lead to improved teaching and student learning. (ibid., p. 101)

Therefore to establish a persistent focus on learning, school leaders might: frequently visit classrooms and participate in professional learning activities with staff, keep up to date with the field and share their learning with others, initiate and guide conversations about student learning, make student learning a focus for performance evaluation, establish teaching and learning as central topics for school-wide staff meetings, analyse data about student learning and use it for planning and work with others to set goals for learning improvement and then review progress in relation to these goals.

School systems and structures to support learning-centred leadership might include planning processes – for lessons, units of work, periods of time, classes and groups of students, and individuals; target-setting – for individuals, groups, classes, years, key stages and the whole school/college; communication systems – especially meetings; monitoring systems – analysing and using student learning data, observing classrooms and providing feedback; roles and responsibilities of leaders – including mentoring and coaching – and policies for learning, teaching and assessment and marking (Southworth, 2009, p. 102).

In order to influence what happens in classrooms in a sustained way, Southworth notes that leaders will be involved in learning at a number of different levels. He speaks of six levels of learning:

1   Pupil learning – *pupils tell us about themselves as learners;*

2   Adult learning – *through joint work, adults teach each other the art and craft of teaching;*

3   Leadership for learning and leadership development – *leaders coach and facilitate others to lead;*

4   School-wide learning – *adults become better every year at supporting pupil learning, just because they work in this school and network;*

5   School-to-school learning – *our schools learn more because they are learning together;*

6   Network-to-network learning – *we feel part of a learning profession.* (Southworth, 2009, pp. 105–7)

When the above levels, structures, systems and processes become embedded and staff collaboration and peer learning become the norm, there will be an 'atmosphere of learning'. Leaders shape organizational cultures but culture is not shaped by school leaders simply saying what should happen, although such descriptions do have a part to play. School culture is more likely to change by headteachers putting in place certain processes and by restructuring the school through specific systems. Leaders bring about re-culturing by restructuring.

The 2002 leadership baseline study found that school leaders that took seriously their learning-centred or instructional role were also concerned to:

> exemplify the qualities of good learners through undertaking themselves continuing professional development, and encouraging and enabling others to do the same. Indeed, becoming one of the school's 'lead-learners' is a distinguishing characteristic of instructional leadership. So, too, is an open-minded, enquiry-based attitude to the education project which thrives on experimentation, not as an end in itself, but rather as the means of developing ever better pedagogical strategies that are selected in order to bring about the positive learning goals the school has for its pupils. (Earley et al., 2002, p. 81)

Similarly, for Levin (2013) working to improve teaching and learning 'must be a central part of everyone's work, every day' and he suggests the need to:

> Build a strong and mutually supportive team of formal and informal leaders in school who encourage and support ongoing learning by staff.

> Ensure that other processes, such as teacher evaluation and student assessment, support rather than detract from learning in the organisation at all levels (for example by not penalising people for trying new things that turn out not to work well).

> Ensure that all of the above is guided by the best available evidence on effective practice in education, including a strong culture of research and evaluation within schools. (2013, p. 7)

Such schools are learning-centred communities where everyone sees themselves as a learner. They also appreciate that professional learning goes on as part of their work – the workplace is a learning workshop. Teachers share their work and collaboratively seek to develop innovative practice since staff believe these to be valuable and productive ways to improve students' learning experiences. They also seize learning opportunities at other sites and events such as conferences, seminars and courses outside the school. Leaders in a learning-centred community promote a strong sense of shared vision for the future; lead the learning, by being seen to be learning with everyone else; and share and distribute leadership and empower others. They also promote collaboration and collegial ways of working and continuous improvement is built into the fabric of the school (Bubb and Earley, 2007).

For the inspection agency Ofsted, two factors make the most difference between successful schools and the rest:

> The first is that they do things consistently well. The second is that leadership is closely involved in making teaching and learning as effective as they can be. This involves leaders modelling effective teaching, evaluating the teaching and learning for which they are managerially responsible, coaching and developing their colleagues, and being accountable for quality. Such leaders are not desk-bound, they are proactive and highly visible around the school. Leadership, in other words, works at a more professional level in focusing on staff learning as well as pupil learning (2012a, pp. 24–5)

How school leaders attempt to operate in this way as learning-centred leaders is described later in the chapter with reference to case studies including one of a new head of inner-city schools who was observed for one day. The next section draws upon the 2012 study to consider the actions leaders take to improve learning in their schools.

Leadership tasks to improve teaching and learning

As part of the survey of the 2012 study into the changing leadership landscape school leaders were invited to list the *three* most important actions that the school was currently taking to lead the improvement of teaching and learning in their area of responsibility. Responses were very individual and wide ranging but the most frequently mentioned are included in Tables 7.1 and 7.2.

For nearly one-fifth of those headteachers replying to this open-ended question, the most important action was more *monitoring* of teaching and learning. Running training/INSET to develop teaching and learning, developing the skills of middle leaders to improve teaching and learning, more/regular lesson observations, and the development of partnerships with other schools were the other main responses (see Table 7.1).

Typical reported actions around teaching and learning included: 'training on good to outstanding', 'increase in number of lesson observations', 'using an external trainer to support the improvement of teaching from good to outstanding' and 'monitoring of learning and teaching including planning and work scrutinies, lesson observations and learning walks'.

For senior/middle leaders, the priorities were, for example, curriculum development/review, monitoring teaching and learning (including with

TABLE 7.1 Important actions to improve teaching and learning – headteachers, 2012

Monitoring teaching and learning (including planning/work scrutinies/use of lesson cameras/action research)	19
INSET/CPD/training related to teaching and learning	17
Developing skills/expertise of middle leaders/ Developing middle leaders roles	15
More/regular lesson observations (with feedback/follow-up)	15
Developing partnership working with other schools	14
Review/Develop assessment procedures/ use of assessment/AfL/APP	11
Mentoring/Coaching	11
Adopt strategies to eliminate inadequate teaching/raise standard to good or better	9
Develop strategies to share outstanding/ good/best practice	9
Curriculum development/adaptation/ review	9
Developing strategies to improve specific area (e.g. writing/speaking + listening)	8
Data analysis/comparisons to inform action/planning/training	8
Pupil progress reviews and interventions	8
Developing senior leaders/SLT roles	7
Peer monitoring/support	7
Use of courses/external training where appropriate – (Masters/NPQH)	6
Working with new Ofsted framework	5
Including teaching and learning in school improvement/ Development plan	5
Restructuring/Modifying performance management procedures/Line management	5
N = 833	

Note: An open-ended question where more than one answer could be put forward. Note that only responses given by 5 per cent or more of respondents are presented in the table. The percentages in this table are weighted by school type and FSM.
Source: Earley et al., 2012, p. 91.

observation), the review of pupil progress, data analysis/comparisons to inform action/planning/training and adopting strategies to eliminate inadequate teaching/raise standard to good or better. Typical responses from senior/ middle leaders concerning curriculum development included: 'embedding creative teaching styles throughout Key Stage 3/4 to meet requirements of new GCSE', 'reviewing primary curriculum provision in our special school', 'developing topic-based learning' and 'to implement a creative curriculum'.

Headteachers had a number of strategies in place to improve teaching and learning in their schools. Data were used extensively, both external (RAISEonline, Fischer Family Trust, benchmarking data provided by the Local Authority [LA]) and internal assessment to enable individual pupil tracking and reporting to parents. Regular progress meetings were common in schools where senior leaders meet with class teachers in primary schools and heads of year or equivalent in secondary schools, to look at individual students' progress, to design interventions and to evaluate the impact of these. Special schools and small primary schools in the 2012 sample noted that national datasets were inapplicable or had limited use, but each had used their own systems and small size to monitor individual pupil progress and set targets.

Many schools were developing teaching learning communities (Wiliam, 2009) and grouping staff for peer observation and mutual challenge and support. Staff were grouped in pairs or triads and, in secondary schools, both within and across subject areas. Several staff were involved in Learning Walks, both senior and middle leaders in most schools and all teachers in some. 'Unannounced' observations, 'drop-ins' or mini-inspections were used in some schools as part of the lesson observation and feedback cycle, running alongside the performance management process. Middle leadership development in providing feedback and challenging poor practice was seen as an integral part of improving teaching and learning across the school. Coaching was mentioned by many schools, with further development of a coaching culture a priority for professional development. The growth in coaching in schools was also earlier noted by the 2007 leadership report (see Chapter 5).

Schools used professional development to improve teaching and learning which was bespoke to the needs of their schools. 'Learn to learn', 'Thinking schools', 'Open schools' provided examples of approaches taken in different schools. All heads were looking for specific expertise, tailored to the needs of their school.

Case studies

The last section of this chapter draws further upon research to illuminate in more detail the actual practice of learning-centred leadership and how schools are trying to keep the focus on learning and teaching, linked to student outcomes. The case studies offer insights into how this focus was demonstrated through the words, deeds, actions, and characteristics of school leaders.

The 2002 baseline study conducted ten case studies of high-performing schools and provided details of activity within each school under the heading of 'instructional leadership'. The case study headteachers held a number of clear – and shared – educational values and beliefs.

> They were principled individuals with a strong commitment to their 'mission', determined to do the best for their schools, particularly for the pupils and students within them. They endeavoured to mediate the many externally-driven directives to ensure, as far as it was possible, that their take-up was consistent with what the school was trying to achieve. (Earley et al., 2002, p. 89)

The same could be said of the leaders of the case study schools described below which are adapted from two National College funded projects – the 2012 landscape study and the 2011 study of new heads in cities. The latter study includes an account of heads 'at work' and how observation can be used as a leadership development strategy.

Leadership landscape

Two examples of improving schools from the 2012 study (Earley et al., 2012, p. 93) are given below: School A, a small, rural primary school and School B, a large secondary academy.

In *School A* the key focus of leadership was on improving the quality and consistency of teaching.

- For pupils this focused on their well-being, attendance and engagement in learning. The school had adopted the international primary curriculum that was seen to support creativity and enjoyment within six-week thematic learning units.

- For teachers, the focus was on monitoring pupil progress and the use of data. This had in part been triggered by Ofsted's recommendations for improvement in the consistency of the teaching of writing and in monitoring progress. Teachers now completed pupil-tracking data that were analysed in pupil progress review meetings with a focus on: underachieving pupils and those not meeting national progress measures. This was combined with book scrutiny on assessment and the establishment of an intervention tracker to enable staff to view the interventions pupils had received during the whole time in the school.

The school had also introduced 'lesson study' that comprised the joint planning and observations of classes by teachers within a key stage or phase. The current focus was on formative assessment. There was also an attempt to develop a school culture or learning atmosphere in which it was 'OK to give constructive criticism'.

Another challenge for the school was to sustain and improve pupil outcomes and the headteacher was developing a whole school approach to focus on building the quality of teaching and learning rather than a continual 'quick fix in Year 6'. This approach included play-based learning and then rigorous and enjoyable learning. There was pressure though to secure results during this process of change.

In *School B* (an academy) following an Ofsted inspection in 2009, a whole school programme of teaching and learning improvement had been developed. Every department had been observed teaching by the senior leadership team (SLT) with the observations reported back to the department heads (HoDs) with subsequent discussion of individual support needs and collective INSET focus. A recurring theme had been assessment for learning (AfL) and differentiation, with teachers often good at focusing on middle- and lower-attaining students, but not so good at stretching higher achievers. This led into a Student Learning Charter, developed with the Student Council, which had a summary of requirements on:

- Lesson planning: (to detail expectations) on lesson preparation and lesson activities such as differentiation, variety of tasks, literacy.

- Lesson delivery: on learning objectives (on what we will learn, rather than what we will do), interactive teaching, starters and a plenary.

- Lesson AfL: on questioning techniques; marking (to reflect: effort, attainment and progress against target).

- Lesson behaviour: on registering of absence; clear seating plans and mutual respect.

- Lesson environment: on having bright, tidy classrooms that display the Student Learning Charter, the rewards policy and Standards of Behaviour policy.

A second phase had focused on a consistency programme in which HoDs went on Learning Walks with an SLT member. An assistant head reported that the SLT had 'tried to change the perception of observations, to feedback positives as well as development priorities . . . but change is never easy for some people'.

A weekly Teaching and Learning support group had also been developed to provide voluntary support: 'by staff for staff'. Focus had included differentiation and use of interactive whiteboards. The principal did not attend these sessions, but was reported to support the initiative.

New heads

Little is known about how headteachers use their time, what they do on a day-to-day basis and how this varies across schools. A report for the National College on *The Experiences of New Headteachers* (Earley et al., 2011) made use, inter alia, of observational methods to gather data on the nature of heads' work. As part of this study six heads were shadowed for a day and their actions recorded using a checklist of activities under six broad headings – leadership, management, administration, teaching, professional development and personal.

A key challenge for all the case study heads was achieving a balance across their various areas of responsibility and ensuring that they focused their time and attention on the things that mattered most. Ensuring time was being spent on the 'right things' and keeping their focus on strategic and learning-centred leadership was a continuing challenge. The case study of one of the six heads is given below. The original observational data (Earley et al., 2011, pp. 78–9) have been re-analysed with reference to the earlier discussion of learning-centred leadership.

Case study

The observed day took place near the end of Rose's first year of headship of a challenging inner-city Church of England primary school. It was a Friday, the last day of a week when the Key Stage 2 tests had been administered. There was a tightly timetabled schedule of events and meetings but it was less busy than usual because Rose and the staff had worked very hard on preparing pupils for the tests, including coming in on the bank holiday. There are 30 people on the staff including 14 teachers, of whom three are newly qualified. Three out of nine classes were not being taught by their regular teacher on the observed day: two teachers were on long-term sick leave and one had been poorly for two days. Two teaching assistants were also away. The school had recently been inspected and was on a 'notice to improve'.

The observation was conducted by Sara Bubb and a summary of her fieldnotes follow:

8.00 a.m.   Administration. Most staff arrive just before the headteacher (HT). Rose chats to office staff and deputy head (DH), in a relaxed but businesslike manner about covering for the three teachers and two teaching assistants who are away. Deals with email in HT's office. [Administration]

8.30 a.m.   Classrooms. Pops into classrooms to chat to teachers as they prepare for the day – very friendly and showing an interest in work. Three out of nine classes are not being taught by their regular teacher today (two are on long-term sick leave and one is poorly today). [Management and LCL – dialogue]

8.45 a.m.   Playground. Talks to the Premises Officer who stands by the gate for security as the school is on a busy street. Greets parents with a big smile saying 'Morning Miss, how are you?' and children with a smile and sometimes a hug. Rose tries to greet parents in their home languages. She says, 'This is an aim for me – it brings a smile to their faces'. Gentle admonishment about a boy eating crisps – mum says he had his breakfast. 8.55 a.m. HT blows the whistle and says good morning to the whole school, they chant good morning back and then walk into class in lines with their teacher. [Management and LCL – dialogue]

9.00 a.m.   Premises management. SBM and premises officer come to HT office to start a health and safety walk around the school. Discuss the CCTV footage of a theft. Focus on the school reception area – where to position the plasma screen and clock to maximise impact on parents, staff and visitors. Discuss improvements to the Early Years outdoor area. [Management and LCL – modelling and dialogue]

9.30 a.m.   Observation of nursery teacher. Rose watches and makes notes, smiling. [LCL – monitoring].

Deals with two brief but urgent interruptions from admin officer about a social services matter. [Management]

9.55 a.m. Administration – letters and emails. Changes from high heels to flat shoes. [Administration]

10.10 a.m.   Meeting with the deputy headteacher who gives feedback on the student teacher's lesson that he has just observed and Rose shares her views on her nursery observation. Very reflective and analytical discussion. [LCL – dialogue and monitoring]

10.30 a.m.   Assembly. The Vicar takes singing assembly with all staff present. Rose sits at back, in the centre and joins in. She moves to front at end to thank the vicar and children, and then dismisses classes but keeps Year 5 and 6 behind for a telling off for not having excellent behaviour. This seems part of a strategy of not loosening the reins on children who might be feeling demob happy after their SATs. [Management and LCL – modelling]

She talks with the vicar about taking pupils to a service in the cathedral. [Management and LCL – dialogue]

11.00 a.m. New disabled child. Meeting through a translator with a Polish mother and her son who has Down's Syndrome and who will be starting school on Monday. Takes them to his reception class to meet staff and children – everyone is pleased to see him and some children give him welcome cards. [Management and LCL – dialogue]

11.15 a.m. Finance management. Reads the post, which has been opened and sorted already by admin staff for ten minutes and then has a scheduled meeting with the school business manager (SBM) and admin officer about buying into the service level agreement with educational psychology service. Discuss school dinner money collecting problems – asking parents to pay off arrears. Raises need for admin officer to keep more detailed records, tracking persistent offenders and speaking to them in the playground. Has set a target to get the arrears down by £500, which the admin officer hasn't met. HT says she needs to see letters and evidence of a staged approach to debt collection. HT makes clear what she needs in an assertive way and stays sitting behind her desk while others sit on lower chairs. The admin officer clearly feeling stressed. [Management]

Goes through attendance figures and what records are being kept. All good news and HT says well done. Tells SBM to monitor admin officer's record keeping more closely. [Management]

Maths consultant pops in for 4 minutes to keep HT updated about progress with the Maths coordinator. [LCL – dialogue]

12.00 p.m. The special needs assistant of the new boy with Down's Syndrome feeds back how he got on and they discuss changing and feeding arrangements with his mother via a translator. [Management]

12.15 p.m. Lunch duty and playground, to stand in for the teaching assistants who are away. Calms children down and gets them lined up. Deals with a play leader. Walks about the dining room and playgrounds – the deputy does this too. Talks to a boy who is upset and has had a fight. Asks the classteacher to sort it out because, 'I don't want to be seen to be the answer to everything'. [Management]

12.45 p.m. Eats lunch in staffroom. She does this a couple of times a week to build relationships 'even though we may be at loggerheads'. [LCL – dialogue]

1.05 p.m.	Rings SBM 'do you have one minute before you go?' even though she's in the office next door, she knocks on the door. Admin task dealt with very professionally. [Administration]
1.30 p.m.	Scheduled meeting about vulnerable children and safeguarding issues with the Inclusion Manager and Learning Mentor. It's very businesslike, focused and no time is wasted. There is a firm message about expecting all staff to ensure that every pupil's needs are being met. They plan case conferences and meetings about statutory assessments. It is clear that Rose is delegating tasks, for example, not attending every meeting. They share information about individuals and processes with external agencies, for example, discussing a new child who is moving from a special school. [LCL – dialogue]
	They review the timetable of the Teaching Assistant for children with English as an additional language to prioritise support for the most needy children. Rose keeps a brief note of key things that need to be done in her notebook and diary, ending positively by saying 'Well done everybody. We're clear what needs to be done'. [LCL – dialogue]
2.15 p.m.	Classrooms. Walkabout for golden time – has a nag of those in detention, shows interest in the activities of all the children and speaks to the teachers. [LCL – dialogue]
2.45 p.m.	Phones a mentor headteacher for about 10 minutes. Shares news and gets advice about wanting her NQT to visit a strong Year 1 teacher. [CPD]
3.00 p.m.	A boy who is leaving the school comes into the office to give Rose a big hug. Very emotional moment: his mother has died so he's moving to live with his grandmother. [LCL – modelling]
3.10 p.m.	Speaks in private to a new teaching assistant about dress code (no denim) as she was wearing jeans. Does so very professionally. [LCL – monitoring] Invites her to the before-school Monday prayer meeting, which the TA seems thrilled about. [LCL – dialogue]
3.15 p.m.	Speaks with parents informally socially in playground. Good PR. Sorts out problems, for example, a mum who feels faint. [LCL – modelling]
3.35 p.m.	Speaks to a teacher about rearranging her assembly date.
3.40 p.m.	Lesson feedback with nursery teacher. [LCL – dialogue]

4.00 p.m.   Reflection on day with deputy. [LCL – dialogue]

4.30 p.m.   Leaves for the weekend. No plans to do more work.

The field note for the day is given below.

Rose was pleased with the day because she achieved everything that she intended to. The schedule was kept to. She has a powerful presence. She conveys a self-assured professionalism that has a very reassuring impact on parents and staff, and this is excellent in terms of public relations as well as in communicating her vision and high expectations. Thus, although some of the tasks done during the observed day might appear to have been simply administrative, they were done with strategic leadership. The time spent in the playground and walking around the school was used for numerous small but powerful interactions with children, parents and staff. Brief conversations with pupils demonstrated a real warmth and interest in them and their learning. It was not possible to speak to this headteacher without being made aware of her very strong belief in the entitlement of every pupil to the very best experience and learning and of her commitment to ensuring this. Learning-centred leadership was thus threaded through all that she did. (adapted from Earley et al., 2011, p. 80)

Using the project's schema for coding activity, the breakdown of Rose's day is shown in Figure 7.2.

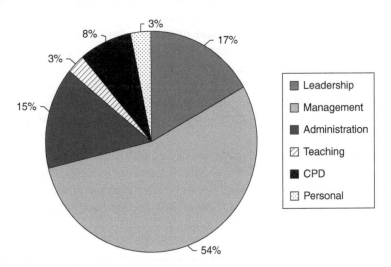

FIGURE 7.2 *Rose's day using categorization of activity (Earley et al., 2011, p. 91).*

Further analysis breaking down her activities according to Southworth's concept of learning-centred leadership shows that much of Rose's time was spent in modelling, monitoring and dialogue – often as part of management tasks.

The observation days were intended to assist the research team to gain information and insights about how headteachers use their time. Although some were initially apprehensive about being observed, all of the headteachers when asked remarked on how valuable they found the experience. It provided them with the 'chance to reflect and think about the issues discussed' and that 'the opportunity to step back and reflect on what has happened and been accomplished is very positive'. The new headteachers valued receiving 'an external perspective on how you do the job, day to day', and being able to step back and think, to stop and take stock and reflect on experiences to date with a fellow professional with no vested interest. Rose found value in articulating and justifying what she was doing: 'Being able to tell myself why I do things as a headteacher in particular ways (and not in others) is critical'. Adding:

> It's a brilliant tool to use for a new head who is moving towards distributive leadership, having more time for leadership work and moving away from management. (Earley et al., 2011, p. 83)

. . . and it might be added, towards learning-centred leadership?

The six case study headteachers' work was fast-paced, stressful and involved a wide variety of activities. They noted that no day was typical which was one of the reasons why the job was deemed to be highly satisfying albeit stressful.

Allocating time in a particular way or doing more of some things (e.g. learning-centred leadership) rather than others (e.g. management) is no guarantee of success. Both are needed for successful schools for as Southworth notes 'too much management and a school may only run smoothly on the spot. Too much leadership and it may be running all over the place and never smoothly!' (2009, p. 101). Nevertheless, as Ofsted remark:

> In schools that are not yet 'good' [an Ofsted category], leadership focuses too much on organisational management and not enough on pedagogy and the leadership of teaching. Heads who are passionate about teaching and encourage others to work at the same level lead good schools. (2012a, p. 6)

Inspection evidence shows 'schools where progress has been rapid, consistent and sustainable demonstrate exceptional *leadership of learning* alongside *strong organisational management*' (p. 19, my italics).

Time spent on learning-centred leadership is key but what is more, as Burkhauser et al., note, 'the quality of actions seems more relevant to outcomes than the amount of time spent' (2012, p. xv). Headteachers must spend time on the things that matter most and acting as a learning-centred leader is a priority for exceptional leaders. An analysis of the six case study headteachers' days provided insights into the things that mattered most, the challenges currently faced and how they were acting (or not) as learning-centred leaders. Certainly the headteachers in the 2011 study seemed to spend more time on 'leadership' including learning-centred leadership and less on administrative activities or organizational management than previous studies found.

Interestingly, the case study headteachers remarked how being observed had been very helpful as it had provided them with the 'chance to reflect and think about the issues discussed'. Feedback on new headteachers' use of time assists them 'to choose to spend time on the right things and spend that time effectively' (Burkhauser et al., 2012, p. 37). Being observed, with feedback which allows opportunities for reflection on practice, is a powerful form of leadership development for all school leaders and not only those new to post (Earley, 2012; Earley and Bubb, 2013).

Summary

How school leaders work to improve teaching and learning was the key focus of this chapter. Effective school leaders – and particularly good leadership of learning – makes the biggest difference to school standards and student performance (Ofsted, 2012a, p. 20). For Levin (2013, p. 6) it is crucial for leaders to:

Build a school climate that makes it clear that everyone in the school is expected to engage in ongoing learning about effective practice (for example through the organisation of effective CPD and the effective use of pupil data to guide improvement), and translate that climate into specific systems and processes that make it an important part of the work of everyone in the school (for example by building discussion of learning into every staff meeting, every school event, every plan, and every major communication).

Leading the learning must be seen as the key responsibility for school leaders and take priority over other competing pressures. However for many not enough time is spent on this crucial activity.

This chapter has drawn upon a range of sources to explore the actions leaders take to improve teaching and learning and create a 'learning atmosphere' or culture. This notion of leadership has gained currency and grown in importance over the period between the first (2002) and most recent landscape studies (2012). The term learning-centred leadership has been unpacked and the most popular strategies for enhancing learning in schools noted, including the monitoring of teaching and learning, offering training to develop teaching and learning, developing middle leaders' skills, lesson observations and the development of partnerships with other schools. Finally, several case studies of 'leading the learning' have been offered including one based on observation. The latter has been noted as an important form of leadership development and it is to this that the next chapter turns.

8

The Training and Development of School Leaders

This chapter draws upon various research studies to consider leadership training and development, preparation for headship, the first year in post and perceptions of necessary future leadership skills and qualities. It looks at the extent to which the skills, capabilities, development needs and support required to lead schools successfully have changed over the past ten years or so. It discusses leadership development provision and what is perceived as effective leadership preparation, development and training. Consideration is also given to the development and training needs of school leaders, how they are currently being met and how they might be met in the future.

The educational landscape has been transformed over our period of study, 2002–2012, 'from one in which schools were very much single units, to the current situation where schools are required to work in partnership with other schools and agencies in order to deliver the best possible outcomes for their pupils' (NC, 2011, p. 11). The Organisation for Economic and Cultural Developments (OECD's) toolkit on *Improving School Leadership* (2009) noted that the changing roles and responsibilities as well as the broader distribution of leadership required headteachers to develop new skills, including 'guiding teaching and learning by enhancing teacher quality that will lead to improved learning outcomes, managing resources, setting goals and measuring progress, and leading and collaborating beyond school borders' (OECD, 2009, p. 19).

Being a school leader in this changing educational landscape is clearly complex but the relevant research literature suggests the challenges have remained broadly similar during our ten-year period, with most of the differences relating to changes in government policy – the ongoing national educational reform agenda and its local implementation. Reduced resources are having an impact on the capacity of Local Authority (LA) to fulfil their former school improvement and development role. Effective leaders need to demonstrate many qualities and traits, including resilience, persistence and emotional, contextual and strategic intelligence – and the need for these has not changed much over the last decade or so, if anything they are needed more than ever! Day et al.'s research suggests that 'a small handful of personal traits explain a high proportion of the variation in leadership effectiveness' (Day et al., 2009, p. 1). There is no single, best fit leadership approach: successful leadership is context sensitive and high-performing leaders possess a range of intelligences, are strategic thinkers and able to 'read' situations and act accordingly. There is a growing understanding of effective leadership practice and the learning and development opportunities needed to help prepare teachers for headship and support them once in post.

Themes and issues are examined in this chapter in a sequential manner, namely as they relate to:

- Preparation and training for becoming a head

- The first year of headship

- Ongoing leadership development

- The skills and qualities needing to be developed.

Preparation and training for becoming a head

The Institute of Education's (IOEs) study for the National College of new headteachers in global cities (Earley et al., 2011) included an extensive review of relevant national and international research that found that the elements of preparation, training and support that school leaders found valuable and the challenges and experiences they typically faced were independent of size or phase of school, culture or geographical location. The problems experienced by newly appointed headteachers were very similar. Many had issues involving relationships, such as dealing with ineffective staff, budgets and financial planning and managing time effectively. Headteachers need to demonstrate many qualities, skills and traits including resilience, persistence and emotional and contextual intelligence. The need to refine, develop and demonstrate these same qualities, skills and traits remain throughout a school leader's career.

The differences largely relate to changes in government policy – responding to the ongoing educational reform agenda. Change management skills are therefore crucial. A leadership challenge for many of the new headteachers in the 2011 study was to know the best time to introduce change given that much change was often seen as needed. Dealing with ineffective staff is a challenge that has been and continues to be faced by new and experienced headteachers in all contexts and cultures. Similarly, knowing 'when to act and when not to act', prioritizing the issues to be addressed and judging the timing of key decisions and actions were key issues and among headteachers' most stressful dilemmas (Earley et al., 2011, pp. 22–3).

Training and development programmes should enable better knowledge and awareness of challenges that headteachers face but research suggests that no amount of experience or preparation – whether through formal training or through experience as a deputy – can provide a sufficient induction to what is a demanding and complex job. Some have argued that it is not feasible or reasonable, to expect headteachers on taking up their first post to possess all the skills, qualities and competences required for effective leadership. However, every effort should be made to prepare them as well as possible and some progress appears to have been made across nations in terms of preparing school leaders for headship (Pont et al., 2009; Huber, 2010).

The issue of preparation for headship was explored in both the 2002 and 2005 leadership studies. In both studies – but unfortunately not in the 2007 or 2012 studies – school leaders were asked how prepared they thought they were *prior* to taking up their current leadership position, and then how prepared they actually were *on taking up* their post. As can be seen from Table 8.1 only a slight improvement had been made between the years with approximately one-third of headteachers in both studies feeling 'underprepared' prior to taking up their first headship, and more feeling that way when in post (44% in 2002, 41% in 2005).

Both the 2002 and 2005 studies found no significant differences in response from male or female heads although secondary headteachers felt better prepared than their primary school colleagues. Neither age of headteacher nor whether they were internal appointments were related to perceptions of adequacy of preparation.

The 2005 study suggested that 'school leaders should not be expected to possess all the skills required for good leadership on taking up their first headship, but learning on the job is a fundamental key skill for school leaders' (Stevens et al., 2005, p. 65). Learning on the job needs to be seen as an essential part of learning to be a headteacher (Earley and Jones, 2009). The 2002 baseline study noted that the most valuable 'on-the-job' activity was working with others, especially an effective headteacher. Everyday work experience, working in a good school with an effective senior leadership team (SLT) and being an acting headteacher were also reported by headteachers to be valuable in their own preparation for headship. The notion of 'Greenhouse

TABLE 8.1 Headteachers' perceptions of how prepared they were for headship – 2002 and 2005

	Very well prepared (%)	Fairly well prepared (%)	Not very well prepared (%)	Not at all prepared (%)
Before headship				
2002 (n = 608)	17	50	25	9
2005 (n = 911)	10	58	23	9
In headship)				
2002 (n = 597)	12	45	35	9
2005 (n = 911)	7	51	30	11

Source: Earley et al., 2002; Stevens et al., 2005.

Schools' and succession planning and leadership development initiatives are described in a number of publications for schools (e.g. NCSL, 2006a, 2007b; Earley and Jones, 2010) and in chains and academies (Matthews et al., 2011; Hill et al., 2012).

The most powerful 'off-the-job' learning reported by headteachers in the 2002 study was undertaking postgraduate programmes. The sustained study and reflection that courses required were seen as very valuable. The 2012 study found that about one-fifth (18%) of headteachers had been involved in university courses and/or university-led action research, with 8 per cent participating in academic study or qualifications (e.g. masters, doctoral study) over the last three years.

Headship qualifications, such as the National Professional Qualification for Headship (NPQH) in England and the Scottish Qualification for Headship (SQH) in Scotland, can aid preparation in many ways, for example, by providing a mentor or coach, practical opportunities for apprenticeship and visits to other schools. The NPQH was first offered in England in 1997 and 'was self-avowedly designed to provide rigorous and above all practical training for senior managers in educational institutions' (Brundrett, 1999, p. 497). It was mandatory for all headship vacancies from April 2004 until April 2012 when the government decided its possession was no longer necessary to become a headteacher. It has had several revisions in the intervening years and in 2013 was part of a wider leadership curriculum consisting of 250 study hours of which 50 are face-to-face. The teaching materials are written at masters levels and include a reflective log. A nine-day placement within another school includes a project designed to raise achievement and to demonstrate impact. Candidates are supported through one-to-one leadership coaching and assessed in a number of ways, including written work, an exam, a case study and an interview. Credits from this 'level 3' qualification can be put towards a higher degree.

For the new inner-city headteachers involved in the 2011 NC research – who all possessed NPQH – features such as providing a coach and visits to other schools contributed to the feeling of readiness to take on the headship role. Other useful aspects of NPQH were found to be opportunities for networking and the strong focus on leadership, with practical sessions on such areas as finance and budget management, HR and legal issues also deemed highly relevant. Stretch assignments and project work which provide 'real-life' insights into headship were also welcomed. These were all found to be part of effective leadership development programmes (Earley and Jones, 2010).

Pre-headship or principal preparation programmes need to develop in participants a number of skills and qualities as well as make them aware of the full range of their responsibilities, including statutory ones such as safeguarding and information about redundancy and capability procedures. They were in favour of NPQH being more practically based as long as there was an appropriate balance between theory and practice. It was felt that the focus on any preparation for a headship qualification should be on learning-centred leadership – how leadership will improve learning, leadership impact or the leadership of learning – and how to influence people to achieve this (see Chapter 7). A number of suggestions to improve NPQH were noted including developing emotional, contextual and spiritual intelligences in individual leaders and ensuring that the importance of situational leadership and its application in their new context is understood. The bespoke or personalized nature of NPQH has been recognized as a strength (Crawford and Earley, 2011) and is still part of the most recent version of the qualification introduced in 2012.

There is no single way of enacting leadership and as models of headship evolve and develop over time it is important that any pre-headship qualification equips new headteachers with the appropriate outlook and skills without it leading to a 'politically-driven intervention to acculturate headteachers and other senior school staff into transformational and distributed leadership' (Wallace et al., 2011, p. 261) which supports politically desired educational reform and ongoing improvement.

International evidence shows clearly that a number of common factors are associated with effective leadership development and principal preparation programmes (Darling Hammond et al., 2009; Earley and Jones, 2010) such as coaching and mentoring, action learning and opportunities for systematic reflection. Being assigned a personal mentor prior to taking up their first headship was considered crucial and has now been recognized through the introduction of various initiatives such as in England the Head Start and Professional Partner schemes. Context is very important in the work of school leaders and although it is possible to speak of headteachers' pre-appointment preparation in general terms, much depends on the setting in which that work takes place. However, learning identified as most helpful during preparation programmes include intellectually challenging elements that help develop reflective practice and integration of theory, values, beliefs and practice which is said to help reduce or minimize the 'culture shock' of taking up a headship. However, no preparation programme will be able to provide headteachers with all the skills they want or need, which is a reminder of the importance of mentoring and other forms of support once in post.

The first year of headship

No matter how good the new headteachers' preparation programmes and their prior experience, a major transition occurs when a school leader takes on a new headship that requires tailor-made or bespoke responses to that particular situation. Formal training programmes such as NPQH increase knowledge and awareness of challenges but no amount of experience or preparation – whether through formal training or through experience as a deputy or acting head – can provide a sufficient induction to what is a demanding and complex job. The role of the 'Professional Partner' (mentor-coach) and other forms of support are important in helping new headteachers to address the context-specific challenges faced including those of 'dealing with place', 'dealing with people', 'dealing with system', and 'dealing with self' (Clarke et al., 2011).

Individual and collective sources of support (e.g. other headteachers, mentors, coaches, networks) should be available to help the new head to develop a cognitive map of the organization using processes of orientation, evaluation (an assessment of staff, understanding where the problems lie) and establishing priorities (Gabarro, 1987). This initial stage of 'entry, orientation and immersion' is when a high proportion of time is spent in understanding the school context and inherited culture and securing initial acceptance and credibility. In this phase new headteachers are concerned with relationship building and increasing self-confidence and self-awareness and acceptance of the need for 'control'. Leading and managing change within their schools will be important and the advice, guidance and support derived from the above sources of great value.

It will also be invaluable to help overcome the loneliness that headship brings and the isolation of the role. These features were frequently recognized pre-appointment but nevertheless come as a shock to some, even internal appointments, on taking up the post. This state of affairs does not appear to have changed significantly over the last 25 years (Weindling and Earley, 1987).

The 2005 and the 2007 leadership studies also stressed the importance of coaching and mentoring. These are now recognized as crucial to the support and development of headteachers, during all phases or stages – preparation, induction, the first few years of headship and towards mid and late career. The personalized and context-specific nature of support and challenge from mentors and coaches is often cited by headteachers – and not only new ones – as being most important. Headteachers may require a range of individuals to call upon: a bespoke service, depending on the issue at stake. The skills and qualities of the individuals providing the mentoring and coaching are deemed to be hugely important, especially the skills to provide a degree of challenge (and support) which pushes them beyond their comfort zone to a new level of awareness and self-confidence (MacBeath, 2011).

The 2011 new headteachers research found that not all school leaders were seen as possessing such coaching and mentoring skills and different mentors were needed at different times for different purposes. Headteachers, both newly appointed and more experienced, needed to be able to access a number of trusted sources they could call on according to the issue in question. The research literature points to the informal, personalized, timely and practical elements of support that were found to be most valuable. The importance of a good match between an experienced head to the context, needs and personality of the new head was found to be extremely important. London's 'Moving to New Headship' (M2NH) programme, for example, spent a lot of time to ensure this worked. There is a growing body of knowledge about how matches of appropriate pairings are optimally formed and of how a good working relationship is best established and maintained. Selection of mentors and the preparation of both mentor and mentees are crucial as a form of leadership development for both parties (Earley et al., 2011).

Headteachers, especially new ones, also benefit from membership of networks, both for practical help (e.g. what to do about an admissions issue) and also for learning and development. Research on new headteachers and outstanding leaders (e.g. West-Burnham, 2009; Walker and Dimmock, 2008) points to the value of headteachers having access to a wide network of fellow professionals, where trust and new learning are developed and knowledge is shared, and which is perceived as more than a support group. MacBeath and colleagues (2009) refer to the importance of supportive networks and regular engagement with other headteachers. Networks – real and virtual – were important in the support and development of headteachers and different networks were used for different purposes.

Leadership development opportunities

Both new and more experienced headteachers need time and opportunities for professional development and reflection and in the context of the ongoing educational reform agenda there are always new things to learn and new initiatives to implement. As headteachers' tenure progresses there will be a continuing need for leadership development, mentoring-coaching, opportunities for reflection and the membership of networks. The development opportunities that school leaders access have been examined in the various leadership studies and it to these that we now turn. The 2012 leadership landscape study asked headteachers whether they had undertaken any professional development (PD) activities specific to their leadership role within the last three years. Ninety per cent of headteachers had done so. However, 8 per cent had not undertaken any leadership development within the last three years.

Where direct comparisons between the different studies are possible there have been significant changes in the take up of various professional development opportunities since 2001. For example:

- More headteachers have undertaken training provided by the local authority (86% in 2012; 74% in 2005; 61% in 2002);

- More headteachers have been mentored by other headteachers (51% in 2012; 46% in 2005; 39% in 2002);

- Fewer headteachers have undertaken training from higher education institutions (8% in 2012; 13% in 2005; 26% in 2002).

In the 2012 landscape survey, of those who had undertaken PD, the highest percentage (86%) participated in activities provided by their Local Authority (LA). A further 84 per cent had attended conferences or seminars, and 58 per cent had engaged in performance management/360 degree feedback. Other activities of note were leadership programmes or courses (56%), networks (55%), mentoring and coaching from others (51%) and regular discussions (51%). Under one-half (44%) of headteachers reported undertaking mentoring/coaching of other school leaders (see Table 8.2).

In order to understand further the 2012 findings statistical analysis was undertaken in relation to phase, school type, Office for Standards in Education (Ofsted) category and free school meal (FSM) eligibility. A number of statistically significant differences were found. For example, headteachers of special schools/Pupil Referral Units (PRUs) were more likely than other headteachers to have undertaken leadership programmes or courses, including commercially provided courses. Secondary school headteachers were also more likely to engage in commercial provision, while primary school headteachers were more likely to be involved in LA and other provision (e.g. chain, diocese) and in induction programmes. Headteachers of schools graded by inspectors as 'outstanding' were more likely to have been involved in leadership programmes or courses (including those of the National College), mentoring and coaching (of others), and job shadowing. Headteachers of 'outstanding' and 'good' schools were also more likely to have been involved in induction programmes as were heads of schools with low percentages of FSM eligible students (Earley et al., 2012, pp. 99–100).

In the 2012 study, senior and middle leaders were also asked about their professional development activity. Only 82 per cent of senior/middle leaders (compared to 90% of headteachers) reported undertaking professional development in the last three years. The range of development activities undertaken by senior/middle leaders was similar to those reported by headteachers. As shown in Table 8.2, 79 per cent of senior/middle leaders participated in LA provision. Two-thirds (67%) engaged in performance management/360 degree feedback, 61 per cent in conferences and seminars, 51 per cent in regular discussions and learning conversation and in leadership programmes or courses, such as those provided by the National College.

Headteachers and senior/middle leaders were also asked to identify the three most effective activities in their own development. Views on the three most effective activities were collected in both the 2002 and 2012 leadership studies, while the 2005 study asked headteachers to comment on the usefulness of the various activities in which they had participated.

In the 2002 baseline study, the top three developmental activities deemed the most effective were conversations with other educationists, local education authority provision, and mentoring from other headteachers (Earley et al., 2002, p. 57). In the 2005 study, headteachers found overall the professional development opportunities taken up in the last three years to be useful, with mentoring from other headteachers (52%), training from education consultants (45%) and development offered by National College for School Leadership (NCSL) (43%) rated as 'very useful' (Stevens et al., 2005, p. 76). Although only 22 per cent of headteachers rated training by local education authorities (LEAs) in this way a further 60 per cent rated it as 'fairly useful'. It was also by far the most common form of professional development or training accessed by headteachers.

TABLE 8.2 Professional development activities in the last three years – headteachers and senior/middle leaders – 2012

	Headteachers (%)	Senior/middle leaders (%)
Local authority provision	86	79
Conferences/seminars	84	61
Performance management/360-degree feedback	58	67
Leadership programmes or courses	56	51
Networks (face-to-face and virtual)	55	43
Mentoring/coaching from others	51	44
Regular discussions (learning conversations)	51	51
Mentoring/coaching of other school leaders	44	31
Other provision (e.g. chain, diocese)	32	16
Collaborative activity (e.g. Teacher Learning Communities)	30	19
Induction programmes	26	19
Other commercial provision	23	14
University provision and/or university-led action research	18	18
Academic study/qualifications	8	14
Job shadowing	5	11
Job rotation	2	6
N	744	645

Source: Earley et al., 2012, p. 100.

Table 8.3 shows the three most effective or beneficial activities in the development of headteachers and senior/middle leaders in the 2012 landscape study. For headteachers these were LA provision (37%), attending

TABLE 8.3 Three most effective development activities, 2012

	Heads (%)	Senior/MLs (%)
Local authority provision	37	42
Leadership programmes or courses e.g. National College	36	41
Conferences/seminars	36	23
Mentoring/coaching from others	29	27
Networks (face-to-face and virtual)	24	19
Mentoring/coaching of other school leaders	19	12
Regular discussions (face-to-face and virtual)	19	23
Collaborative activity (e.g. Teacher Learning Communities)	14	6
Performance management/360 degree feedback	13	29
Other provision (e.g. chain, diocese)	12	6
Other commercial provision	10	7
University provision and/or university-led action research	5	6
Academic study/qualifications (e.g. masters, doctoral study)	4	9
Induction programmes	4	5
Job rotation	1	3
Job shadowing	1	5
N	737	642

Note: More than one answer could be put forward so percentages may sum to more than 100. The percentages in this table are weighted by school type, size and FSM.
A filter question: all those who ticked 'yes' to undertaking professional development activity specific to their leadership role.
Source: Earley et al., 2012, p. 102.

conferences/seminars and leadership programmes or courses (both 36%). Also of benefit were mentoring/coaching from others (29%) and networks (24%), both face-to-face and virtual. About four-in-ten middle/senior leaders indicated LA provision (42%) and the use of leadership programmes or courses (41%) were one of their three most effective activities.

No one developmental activity was considered extremely beneficial, despite several activities, such as LA provision and conferences/seminars, emerging as prominently used.

The 2012 study also revealed a number of statistically significant differences among respondents. Perhaps unsurprisingly, academy headteachers were least likely to make reference to LA provision and primary headteachers the most likely. Secondary school headteachers were more likely than other heads to refer to 'other commercial provision' and 'conferences and seminars' as among their three most effective PD activities (Earley et al., 2012, p. 102).

In summary, there were clear similarities across the studies from 2002 to 2012 of leaders' views on effectiveness: mentoring, training by consultants, and LAs were consistently mentioned. Networking (both face-to-face and virtual) and other forms of collaborative activity have become more important over the decade.

Skills and qualities to be developed

Both the 2002 and 2012 studies asked respondents to reflect on the leadership skills and qualities they most needed to develop over the next 18 months. The 2002 baseline study made use of the existing national standards for headteachers (DfEE, 1998) and the three standards where further training and development opportunities were most commonly welcomed, were to:

- 'promote and secure good teaching, effective learning and high standards of achievement' (58% of headteachers and 49% of deputies);

- 'agree, develop and implement systems to meet the learning needs of all pupils' (47% of headteachers and 32% of deputies);

- 'keep the work of the school under review and account for its improvement' (44% of headteachers and 32% of deputies).

The only standard where there was a considerable phase difference was 'lead, support and co-ordinate high quality professional development for all staff, including your own personal and professional development', more primary headteachers (49%) than secondary (30%) saw this as a priority area. The standard 'promote and secure good teaching, effective learning and high standards of achievement' also had phase differences but with more secondary heads requesting training and development.

In the 2012 landscape study headteachers' development needs often reflected what they had identified as their most significant leadership challenges (see Chapter 4). As shown in Table 8.4, resulting development needs included 'strategies for closing attainment gaps' (49%), 'developing future leaders of succession planning' (46%), 'leading curriculum change and innovation' (46%), 'modelling excellence in the leadership of teaching and learning' (37%) and 'forming partnerships with schools and agencies to improve outcomes' (37%). Interestingly, only a quarter of headteachers highlighted 'managing finances and premises' as a skill area that needed to be developed despite financial and budgeting issues being the leadership challenge most frequently mentioned (see Chapter 4). This may be because many schools, particularly secondary and large primary, have business managers or bursars who lead on such matters.

A number of statistically significant differences emerged in the 2012 study. Headteachers from schools graded by inspectors as 'outstanding' and those with the lowest proportion of FSM eligible pupils were less likely to refer to 'strategies for closing attainment gaps' and to 'engaging with parents and the local community' as a development need. Headteachers of 'outstanding' and 'good' schools were also least likely to refer to 'modelling excellence in the leadership of teaching and learning' and 'marketing your school'. Headteachers of 'outstanding' schools, however, as well as those from special schools, were more likely than others to refer to 'providing services or support to other schools or organisations' as a skill that required development.

Primary school headteachers were most likely to refer to 'developing personal resilience', 'strategies for leading professional development' and 'purchasing services from a range of suppliers'. Head of special schools and PRUs were most likely to refer to 'analysing and interpreting student data and information', 'implementing change and improvement successfully' and 'developing future leaders and succession planning'. Interestingly, headteachers from schools with the highest percentage of FSMs were least likely to refer to 'strategic thinking and scanning to anticipate trends' as development needs (Earley et al., 2012, pp. 102–3).

In 2012 senior/middle leaders identified 'leading curriculum change and innovation' (46%) and 'modelling excellence in the leadership of teaching and learning' (41%) as their greatest areas for development. They had more emphasis on teaching, learning and pupil outcomes than headteachers, reflecting their responsibilities and roles.

Mention was made earlier to workplace learning and 'growing your own leaders'. Such learning and development is acquired through living

TABLE 8.4 Leadership skills and qualities most needed over next 18 months, 2012

Which, if any, of the following leadership skills and qualities do you think you most need to develop over the next 18 months?	Head (%)	SL/ML (%)
Strategies for closing attainment gaps	49	52
Leading curriculum change and innovation	46	46
Modelling excellence in the leadership of teaching and learning	37	41
Forming partnerships with schools and agencies to improve outcomes	37	33
Implementing change and improvement successfully	33	38
Strategic thinking and scanning to anticipate trends and political agendas	29	36
Marketing your school	28	23
Developing an entrepreneurial ethos within your school leadership	28	21
Analysing and interpreting student data and information	26	40
Developing personal resilience	25	24
Knowing your legal responsibilities as a school leader	24	34
Developing a learning culture and organization community	22	13
Using learning theories and pedagogies to influence teaching	22	22
Engaging and building effective relations with parents and the community	19	20
Strategies for leading professional development	13	21
Adapting your leadership style to the school's culture and needs	12	17
Developing effective project management skills	9	13
Developing interpersonal skills	4	9
N	833	769

Note: More than one answer could be put forward so percentages may sum to more than 100. The percentages in this table are weighted by school type and FSM eligibility.
From a filter question: all those who ticked 'yes' to undertaking professional development activity specific to their leadership role.
Source: Earley et al., 2012, pp. 103–4.

the experience while in the role and this re-emphasizes the importance of headteachers as people developers of leaders – what Collins (2001) referred to as 'level 5' leaders. To plan for leadership development and succession, headteachers in 2012 commonly reported building this into their way of working. This often began at recruitment, with time invested to select high-quality teachers with leadership potential and by asking about leadership ambitions at interview. Performance management was also used – 'we always ask staff where they want to be in five years' – and aspirations identified through performance reviews were commonly said to be supported through development opportunities. Examples specifically mentioned in the 2012 study included:

- Providing opportunities to take responsibility within the school, for example, through bursaries, rotating subject coordination and/or giving responsibility for leading curriculum initiatives;

- Staff working alongside or to support other schools, in leadership roles or as an Advanced Skills Teacher (AST), with the new Specialist Leader of Education (SLE) role being mentioned in some cases;

- Leadership courses provided through external providers, such as National College programmes or local variants of these;

- Courses provided by other national training networks;

- Visiting other schools to see good practice;

- Providing an accreditation route for support staff, to provide a ladder of opportunity;

- Opportunities to gain Masters awards, for example, school-based programmes delivered by Higher Education Institutions (HEIs). (Earley et al., 2012, p. 106)

It was considered important that, alongside real opportunities to take a lead responsibility, there was the availability of coaching and support. New opportunities, such as those offered by becoming a Teaching School, were also seen to provide new ways in which to develop leadership skills of staff.

Summary

This chapter has identified the main research findings from various studies over the period 2002–12 relating to leadership preparation, development and training for school leaders. Recurring themes included: the importance of work-based development, pre-appointment training, support networks, coaching and mentoring, and opportunities for reflection. The main sources of professional development and perceptions of their value appeared to have changed little over time but the future was more problematic. External support and advice that school leaders currently draw upon and especially how these may alter within a changing educational landscape were discussed in Chapter 2. Here it was noted how the traditional role of the LA was changing and while some headteachers, especially those from primary schools, recognized their LA as an effective and beneficial service which they wished to retain, others were less complimentary. Some were diversifying by forming partnerships or alliances to facilitate and sustain aspects of the LA improvement and development services. Others were looking to Teaching Schools and their alliances as new forms of support, training and development and many heads predicted they would be using a wider range of providers in 18 months' time, including those that few schools currently use or consider important. These findings suggest a greater diversity in training, development and support but also uncertainty as schools anticipated moving away from the known and the well used. It is the future of leadership in this ever-changing scenario that is the focus of the final chapter.

9

Future Challenges and School Leadership

In the evolving educational policy landscape, the challenges and complexity of school leadership, and headship in particular, continue to increase with a consequent intensification of work. The need to develop internal school capacity and effective partnerships with appropriate external support, appear essential for schools as they face challenges and navigate numerous national policy changes, within their own particular contexts. Over the course of the four leadership studies from 2002 to 2012, some of the challenges have remained largely unchanged: the need for change and improvement appears a permanent part of the landscape. There is a clear risk, however, that the nature and demands of current policy will disrupt the focus of schools and leaders from teaching and learning and authentic improvement. There are signs that potential fault lines could be emerging between leaders across school phases, contexts and inspection gradings. These fault lines include not only school capacity, but also the ways in which school leaders view the potential impact of new policies and challenges and respond to them.

This chapter therefore deals with several interrelated issues that are likely to present challenges and impact on the future of school leaders and leadership, and by implication the success of the education system. These are:

- the intensification of leadership roles and the importance of distributed leadership;

- support for schools and the role of the middle tier;

- the move towards a self-improving school system;

- leading the learning; and

- the importance of leadership development for the future.

It concludes by re-emphasizing the key role that leaders play in school success and therefore the need to ensure that in an increasingly devolved system adequate resources continue to be devoted to their support and development.

The intensification of leadership and its distribution

John MacBeath and colleagues (2012) writing about coping strategies among Scottish headteachers provide a helpful account of what it means to be a headteacher in the third millennium. They refer to the Pont et al., (2008) Organisation for Economic and Cultural Development (OECD) six-nation study that talks about a changing and challenging environment where heads and schools are being given an even bigger job to do:

> Greater decentralisation in many countries is being coupled with more school autonomy, more accountability for school and student results, and a better use of the knowledge base of education and pedagogic processes. It is also being coupled with broader responsibility for contributing to, and supporting, the schools' local communities, other schools and other public services. (Pont et al., p. 60)

These are common themes in the literature and for MacBeath and colleagues a good descriptor of what it means to be a headteacher in the 2010s is 'intensification': 'increasing pressure to do more in less time, to be responsive to a greater range of demands from external sources and to meet a greater range of targets, accompanied by impatient deadlines to be met' (2012, p. 422). Fink summed it up well when he said headteachers were reporting being overburdened, overworked and overwhelmed (2010, p. 35).

Yet it need not be like this. In fact, the hours headteachers work during term time – between 55 to 60 – have not changed considerably over the last decade (see Chapter 6) despite government attempts to address issues of workload and work-life balance. The key question is how that time is spent. Headteachers are frequently unable to spend appropriate time on the things that matter. Too much time is spent on tasks that might be better delegated elsewhere in order to enable school leaders to concentrate on key tasks and activities. Many schools are now deploying school business managers and other specialists to enable them to focus on other activities. Also it is the quality of actions taken rather than amount of time allocated to different actions per se that is important and 'spending time on one issue or area in and of itself does not lead to success. A principal must choose to spend time on the right things and spend that time effectively' (Burkhauser et al., 2012, p. 37).

What 'the right things' are has been the subject of much debate over the years as headteachers become more like chief executives running a business and less like leading professionals running a school, a trend identified in the 1970s by Meredith Hughes (Hughes, 1976). Schools have increasingly been recognized as autonomous businesses yet, as discussed in Chapter 7, that core business should be 'learning'. Ben Levin (2013, p. 5) writing about 'confident leadership' suggests that school leaders are currently expected to have too many skills, 'making the task seem impossible for ordinary mortals'. While many skills matter, he believes that:

> To be truly confident about their work school leaders need to feel capable in two major areas: leading teaching and learning, and being able to manage the political environment in and outside the school in a way that sustains the organisation and builds community support for it. (Levin, 2013, p. 5)

As noted earlier for Levin leading learning is the key responsibility, to which leaders need to devote much time and give priority over competing pressures (Levin, 2013).

School leaders continue to face many challenges – the need to raise standards, rising expectations from government, inspectors, parents and pupils, a highly diverse school population, a changing curriculum and so on – and these challenges are unlikely to go away. The roles of and expectations for school leaders are changing continuously and as the task of leading a school has grown and become more complex, it has become increasingly apparent that the expectations of principals far exceeds what one individual alone can achieve. It is no longer possible or desirable for the headteacher to lead on everything – principals can't do it alone – and the leadership of key tasks needs to be distributed to those with the appropriate expertise. As Hallinger notes 'sustainable school improvement must be supported by leadership that is shared among stakeholders' (2012, p. 13). Neither should leadership be confined to those in official positions. The leadership of learning, for example, is everybody's responsibility.

There is more shared leadership. Senior/middle leaders in the 2012 study felt involved to some degree in all areas of school leadership and were most likely to be very involved in setting aims and objectives of the school and monitoring and evaluating progress against them. They felt most involved in influencing whole-school decisions that impacted on their responsibilities, followed by influencing whole-school approaches to teaching and learning, mentoring and supporting teachers and helping to make strategic decisions.

In this context of work intensification and the perceived impossibility of doing this ever expanding job, it is perhaps unsurprising that few people are putting themselves forward as the next generation of headteachers. There is now considerable evidence to suggest that potential headship candidates hesitate to apply for posts due to the extensive responsibilities associated with the role, growing accountability demands, inadequate preparation, training and support and insufficient rewards or salary differentials (Earley and Jones, 2009).

In the 2012 study heads commonly reflected on leadership succession challenges and the lack of appetite for staff to take on senior leadership and headship roles. Although this was not always the case in their own schools, many heads commented that this was frequently across their wider networks. Staff were reported to be 'turned off' by increasing expectations and high levels of accountability where headteachers were deemed to be only as good as their last inspection report and hence felt they were subject to dismissal as the 'buck stopped with them'. This was especially the case in challenging schools where the pressures to succeed and to succeed rapidly were said to be putting off talented people from applying (Lightman, 2013).

However, headteachers themselves are still often of the view that it is the best job in education – and this has not changed very much over the years (Earley and Weindling, 2004; Weindling and Earley, 1987) – but some were less certain about the future direction headship was taking given recent policy developments. Headship had often been seen as 'a work of passion' but some heads in the 2012 study were no longer sure whether it was as alluring and appealing as before. Headteachers were often seen as being very vulnerable, particularly in relation to the Office for Standards in Education (Ofsted) inspection framework which presented challenges at all levels: whether you were a leader of a 'poor', a 'need for improvement' or an 'outstanding' school. Others saw the role of headteacher as becoming increasingly like a CEO and commented that 'that's not what I went into leadership to do'. Academies, chains and federations were perceived to be taking over the role of the Local Authority (LA), a development that not all welcomed, especially primary school heads. As discussed in Chapter 2, this also had implications for the sources of support available to heads and other school leaders both now and in the future.

Support for schools and the role of the middle tier

The sources of support for schools and their leaders in the future is a further challenge. It is not always clear where such support is to come from in an evolving landscape that includes a wide range of organizational structures and a strong central drive towards academisation, with resulting effects on local authorities and their resources. Academies, federations and chains are growing in number and size, with some of them taking on many of the functions once undertaken by LAs. Local authorities are also required to adapt to this landscape where they are seen as one of many potential middle tiers (academy chains, federations, national organizations, etc) with which schools may choose to engage. As Smith (2012, p. 19) notes:

> This is at a time in which there is uncertainty about the extent to which LAs will be able to sustain a significant school support infrastructure as resources are increasingly invested directly in schools (including academies). This raises clear questions about LAs' roles, specifically the extent to which they will be responsible for school standards at a time when they are playing a diminishing role in the middle tier.

Local authority performance and practice, historically, is variable (Ofsted, 2012a) and many are, understandably, finding it difficult to perform their school improvement role, given the redistribution of resources to academies. Indeed, the Royal Society of Arts Academies Commission report (2013) goes as far as to say that schools themselves increasingly need to provide school improvement services to other schools and that LAs' role should be restricted to planning and commissioning school places to meet local need and to champion the needs and interests of all children in the area. Smith is broadly supportive of this when he notes that:

> What LAs do offer is the stability of a durable, recognised entity that has the potential to maintain an overview of local needs and provision. At the same time, they offer a means of focusing on the broad moral purpose of the education system by maintaining a strategic overview in a way which may not be possible for other forms of middle tier. (2012, p. 19)

For Levin (2013) the diminishing role of LAs has also 'removed a more senior level of leadership that exists in other systems, who can support individual school leaders and also speak more effectively to regional and national issues' (2013, p. 13).

Interestingly, Smith suggests that:

> The most compelling case for ensuring that the middle tier role is undertake by LAs or municipalities is related to the degree of permanence which they offer in a system in which they contribute to schools' work alongside dynamic networks which may be more fluid and transient in nature. (2012, p. 21)

In the rapidly changing landscape of the mid-2010s such a degree of permanence or stability would be welcomed by many as they seek to partner with others and find appropriate systems of support and challenge. Evidence from the 2012 study suggests there is a danger of a polarized system developing between those schools that are well connected and supported and those that are not. In a system that is rapidly changing and continuously presenting new demands to schools, those that lack access to the necessary sources of support will be seriously disadvantaged. While some school leaders welcomed access to a wider pool of support and development services, for most it was unclear whether this patchwork of provision would provide appropriate and equitable support.

For schools to improve they need to have robust and challenging discussions both internally and with outside agencies. The changing role of Ofsted with its greater emphasis of supporting schools in need of improvement (Ofsted, 2012a) and the support, evaluation and review offered by such peer-led groups as the Challenge Partners (www.challengepartners.org.) are interesting developments worthy of further research. As Smith notes professional networks and peer support offer different models 'to market- or competition-based models (Pont et al., 2008; Chapman and Hadfield, 2009) in which the best schools flourish solely on the basis of their own innovation and success' (2012, p. 5). However, it is not always clear how the potential tension between partnership and cooperation, and school choice and competition can be resolved. With the anticipated decline of many LA functions, government policy argues that schools will gain support from a mixed economy and operate within a climate of 'co-opetition' – a neologism coined to describe cooperative competition. Only time will tell how successful this proves to be.

Towards a self-improving school system

In England, in recent years the educational landscape has shifted from one in which schools were very much single units to where more partnership working is required. Smith (2012) notes how the educational landscape has been transformed over the last decade or so 'as established structures that traditionally promoted school improvement have given way to a more fluid system based on school-focused networks' (p. 3). In an era of growing school autonomy, academisation and diminishing local authority support, the need for schools to work in a more collaborative manner is greater than ever, although they still must compete for pupil admissions and staff. A self-improving system involves identifying the challenges and encouraging collaborative working between schools in order to tackle them.

Schools are now expected to lead their own improvement (DfE, 2010a) with limited or no local authority support. The coalition government stated:

'Our aim should be to support the school system to become *more effectively self-improving'* (DfE, 2010a, p. 13). The National College who have been charged with driving this process state:

> The self-improving system can be defined as one in which schools themselves, through greater autonomy and freedom, are in the driving seat of school improvement and professional development, working together to spread best practice, knowledge and experience to the benefit of schools across the system. (NC, 2013, p. 4)

One key issue, however, is that the concept of a self-improving system 'has become synonymous in some quarters with academisation and other structural solutions' (NC, 2013, p. 11). The report from the Academies Commission (2013) was clear that academy status alone was not a panacea for improvement, reminding us that all kinds of schools and colleges can be successful – and all kinds can underperform.

School-to-school support is being encouraged through a type of school leader, known generically as 'system leaders' which includes National, local and specialist leaders of education (NLEs, LLEs and SLEs). Previous national strategies for school improvement such as the literacy strategy have been abolished. System leaders exercise leadership beyond their own schools, sharing their expertise and their school's practice with other less-effective schools through school improvement partnerships. The best school leaders 'are working to build robust partnerships between schools so that teachers learn from and with each other; and capacity is shared so that pupil outcomes are improved' (NC, 2013, p. 3).

System leaders also have an important role in supporting and complementing the teaching schools approach (similar to teaching hospitals) and the first cohort of Teaching Schools was designated in summer 2011. National, Local and Specialist Leaders of Education and the creation of a national network of Teaching Schools and TSAs are potentially powerful drivers of school-led improvement (Hargreaves, 2010, 2011, 2012). There is a growing body of evidence showing the benefits of such an approach (e.g. Hill and Matthews, 2008, 2010). School improvement was found to be most effective when:

> an able and committed school leader is paired with the leader of a struggling or underperforming school and involves his or her home school in this relationship and the task of achieving change and improvement. (Hill and Matthews, 2008, p. 24)

Similar findings were noted in the first evaluation of the school improvement initiative, London Challenge, where the notion of 'consultant leaders' was adopted (Earley and Weindling, 2006). However, even under plans to develop 500 TSAs up to a half of all schools in England may be left out (Hill, 2012, p. 22). Similarly, the RSA report on academies shows that many school leaders of converted academies are not working with other schools as originally envisaged (Academies Commission, 2013). It is early days of course and as we saw in Chapter 2 some heads are undecided or uncertain about Teaching Schools and related developments. They were reluctant to engage so it will be interesting to see how policy develops over the next five years or so. There is the very real danger that the gap between the best schools and the rest could widen:

> There is a risk of a two-tier system emerging in which some schools gain significantly from the enhanced continuing professional development (CPD), the sharing of expertise and peer evaluation and challenge that comes from working with other schools, while others find themselves increasingly isolated. (NC, 2013, p. 3)

At a national level the self-improving system is not yet fully in existence but there are small sub-systems, largely built around Teaching Schools and their alliances, chains and federations, proving that as a concept it is possible. Whether it expands or not from its current state remains to be seen and will depend on a number of educational and political factors. An education system in which some schools are left behind, or disenfranchised as a consequence of not feeling a part of this 'self-improving system' is a very real possibility. The new educational landscape should be about identifying the challenges and encouraging collaboration between schools in order to tackle them and achieve system success.

Leading the learning

As was noted in Chapter 7 for Levin school leaders have to 'identify the work of leading learning as a key responsibility, to which they devote a considerable amount of time and attention and which takes priority over other competing pressures' (2013, pp. 5–6). This may be easier said than done however, and for some in the 2012 study the nature and demands of current policy were seen as potentially disrupting the focus of schools and leaders from teaching and learning and their authentic improvement. In particular, among smaller secondaries and many primary schools there was considerable concern that additional managerial powers and duties would disrupt a leadership focus on learning at the same time when the normal channels of support were missing.

Achieving real improvement or change in schools, as discussed in Chapter 7, requires a focus on learning-centred leadership with priority given to enhancing teaching and learning. The leadership of learning, for example, was seen as everybody's responsibility and school leaders needed to help foster a culture of learning for all. An emphasis on organization structures and new forms of schooling may be distracting from this key objective. For stand-alone schools vulnerable to LA decline, additional autonomy over finance, human resources and the procurement of services could appear as unwanted burdens that bear little relevance to learning. The 2012 study reported that the most common challenge faced was reductions in funding followed by the new Ofsted inspection framework. Academy status and sustaining/improving student outcomes (particularly attainment) were also noted as concerns. Notably, less than 10 per cent of each group of school leaders identified directly improving the quality of teaching and learning.

The last is an important point and over the next decade or so it is most likely that leaders, especially headteachers, will be increasingly extolled to become leaders of learning (e.g. Ofsted, 2012a). The OECD's toolkit on *Improving School Leadership* (2009) notes that leaders play a key role in improving school outcomes by influencing the motivation and capacity of teachers and affecting the climate and environment in which they work and learn. Can we detect a growing expectation that headteachers as well as other school leaders will maintain this focus – to concentrate their efforts on professional and pedagogic matters rather than administrative and financial concerns? As noted earlier, schools have made a number of efforts, including the growth and deployment of administrative staff, especially school business leaders, to help maintain this leadership focus on enhancing student outcomes. The evidence does suggest, however, that it is becoming increasingly difficult to maintain the focus on the leadership of teaching and learning – in 2012, 58 per cent of headteachers reported that they spent 'too little time' on this activity although four out of ten said the time spent was 'about right'.

The 2012 Ofsted annual report makes this point very clearly. It is the leadership of teaching and learning that makes the biggest difference to school standards and 'outstanding schools strive to create a culture and ethos where professional dialogue about learning and teaching is highly valued and forms part of the fabric of the school' (2012a, p. 20). This, Ofsted claims, is the basis of a learning community. A learning-centred school is going to be led by learning-centred leaders (Bubb and Earley, 2010) and according to the OECD such leaders operate in four main ways:

By monitoring and evaluating teacher performance; conducting and arranging for mentoring and coaching; planning teacher professional development; and orchestrating teamwork and collaborative learning. (OECD, 2009, p. 12)

Ofsted is clear on this matter when it notes that leadership in schools that are not yet 'good' concentrates 'too much on organisational management and not enough on pedagogy and the leadership of teaching' (2012a, p. 6).

The biggest difference to school standards is related to the effective leadership of teaching and learning and Ofsted believes that the most important differences between highly effective schools and the rest is that they do things consistently well and that the leadership is closely involved in making teaching and learning as effective as possible:

> This involves leaders modelling effective teaching, evaluating the teaching and learning for which they are managerially responsible, coaching and developing their colleagues, and being accountable for quality. Such leaders are not desk-bound, they are proactive and highly visible around the school. Leadership, in other words, works at a more professional level in focusing on staff learning as well as pupil learning. (Ofsted, 2012a, pp. 24–5)

Learning-centred leadership or leadership for learning has become and is likely to continue to be the new paradigm for twenty-first century school leadership (Hallinger, 2012, p. 2), yet in the 2012 study just over one-half of headteachers' time was spent in the office and just over one-third inside the school (but outside the office). It is acceptable and realistic to expect school leaders – all leaders and not only headteachers – to adopt this model of school leadership but it is difficult to fulfil if so much time is spent 'office-bound'. Given its greater prominence in the inspection framework for English schools there is a good chance that it will happen ('what gets inspected gets done') but it will be a challenge given the intensification trend noted earlier and the growing number of competing pressures and demands on school leaders' time.

Leadership development and the future

The OECD's leadership reports (Pont et al., 2008; OECD, 2009; Schleicher, 2012) note that school leadership has become a priority development area in many of its member countries. Its investigation of 22 educational systems in 19 countries considers different countries' approaches to enhancing the quality and sustainability of school leadership.

It identified four policy levers which, taken together, can improve school leadership practice, namely:

1 (Re)defining school leadership responsibilities

2 Distributing school leadership

3 Making school leadership an attractive profession

4 Developing skills for effective school leadership

The first three have already been discussed and regarding the latter, in England, we have seen over the course of the last few decades considerable development in this area. Simkins (2012) provides an excellent overview of how leadership and management development provision in England has changed with a move from relatively limited and fragmented provision to one, until recently, of the most centralized forms in the world. He refers to three distinct eras of school leadership with associated training and development. From 1944 to the mid-1980s was the era of *Administration*, when teachers had high degrees of autonomy and the work of headteachers was seen as being both 'lead professionals' and administrators. Hughes developed the notion of 'professional-as-administrator', a hybrid notion that saw the head 'seeking accommodation between the complex and sometimes conflicting sub-roles of "leading professional" and "chief executive" (Hughes, 1976), a distinction that pre-figured key aspects of the debates of the later eras' (Simkins, 2012, p. 623).

The second era of *Management*, from the mid-1980s to 1997, was marked by increasing government concern about standards and the performance of schools. Administrators were now more likely to be seen as 'managers' who were made responsible for their school's performance against government defined criteria. Simkins' third era of *Leadership*, began in 1997 with the election of New Labour and their 'modernization' agenda. This built on the managerial framework of school autonomy and accountability but added 'leadership' which was seen as:

> providing a much stronger agentic thrust in instituting change and improving performance in the public sector in general and schools in particular than the more conservative idea of 'management' . . . This move was embodied in the establishment of the National College for School Leadership in 2000. (Simkins, 2012, p. 625)

The National College for School Leadership (NCSL) provided both greater policy influence over and coherence to the provision of leadership training and development.

Since the establishment of the NCSL in November 2000, the training and development of educational leaders has been high on the policy agenda (Earley and Evans, 2004), with most recently, in 2012, the creation of a 'leadership curriculum' made up of five levels and including national professional qualifications for middle leaders, senior leaders and headteachers. Leadership development is increasingly seen as a process of lifelong learning with leaders requiring both formal and informal support processes throughout the different stages of their careers.

Effective leaders do not just emerge, for as Levin has noted they must

> be developed and cultivated. Leadership recruitment and development must be a key part of any successful improvement strategy . . . However, leadership development is not an end in itself; it is only a means by which goals can be achieved. (2012, p. 18)

The question of which educational goals – or leadership for what? – is an interesting one but beyond the scope of this book. Cranston (2013, p. 130), among others, has argued for the need to challenge the orthodoxy of school leadership being for student learning when the learning is defined in such narrow (academic) terms and measured by national and international testing programmes. Schooling is about much more and school leaders, he argues, should be critically examining the process of learning and that 'the constraints of accountability on school leaders need to be replaced by a new liberating professionalism for school leaders framed around notions of professional responsibility' (p. 130). In Simkin's (1997) terms while the operational power of school leaders continues to increase, criteria power have become much more a central government concern and away from school leaders and teachers. Similarly, Hoyle and Wallace's (2007) 'principled infidelity' and Gold et al.'s (2002) 'principled principals' (see Chapter 2) may be becoming more difficult to enact.

The 2012 study found school leaders commonly considered the goals of schooling to remain tightly held by central government. As noted in Chapter 2, in areas where government claimed new autonomies for schools, for example, over parts of the curriculum and assessment, many schools reported further refinements to central control, for instance through new definitions of measures of success. Change was perceived in a way that sustained government control including through the definition of standards, inspections and intervention.

The OECD (2009) leadership toolkit talks of strengthening practice through leadership development and that the broader distribution of leadership and headteachers' changing roles and responsibilities require the development of new skills for the twenty-first century. These include:

> Guiding teaching and learning by enhancing teacher quality that will lead to improved learning outcomes, managing resources, setting goals and measuring progress, and leading and collaborating beyond school borders. (2009, p. 19)

There is however no single best way to provide leadership development opportunities but learning at the workplace should complement formal learning (Earley and Jones, 2009). As the OECD toolkit asserts, training and development programmes must include an appropriate balance of theoretical and practical knowledge and self study and include research about effective leadership learning. It notes that:

> Different types of skills are needed for leading in certain contexts, it is increasingly accepted that there is a set of leadership constructs that are broadly applicable across cultures as long as cultural values, behaviours and sensitivity to context are applied as they are used. (2009, p. 21)

Interestingly, research on effective educational leaders conducted by the McKinsey Corporation for the National College (Barber et al., 2010), notes that most of the international evidence suggests that 'good leadership is the same irrespective of context, and that "what works" is surprisingly consistent. For instance, the literature review found remarkably similar traits and practices in effective school leaders from Australia to Pakistan to Africa' (ibid., p. 3). They highlight a set of practices that effective leaders share, and a common set of beliefs, attitudes, and personal attributes which they possess. It is important therefore that any training and development opportunities offered are able to promote and develop such aspects of leadership.

In England, as in many other education systems, the ever-changing policy agenda, the ever-rising bar of school performance, as defined, for example, by inspection frameworks, necessitate an effective system of leadership development and training to develop new skills and competences and refine existing ones. Leaders and their schools require continuing development and support to lead their schools into the twenty-first century. However, they need to 'position themselves as proactive reflexive leadership professionals, not reactive managers' (Cranston, 2013, p. 139) responding to others' agendas and complying with external mandates.

Another OECD report has emphasized the need for education systems to help *students* become lifelong learners and to:

> manage complex ways of thinking and working and being capable not only of constantly adapting but also of constantly learning and growing, of positioning themselves and repositioning themselves in a fast changing world. (Schleicher, 2012, p. 11)

The same is equally true of educational leaders as they face a growing number of challenges of increasing complexity. The importance of effective leadership development therefore should not be underestimated. This should include the opportunity for self-reflection and be a more customized or personalized type of training and leadership development, 'where (headteachers) have the opportunity to shape their own professional development' (Stroud, 2006,

p. 94) *and* professionalism – as proactive leadership professionals (Cranston, 2013, p. 139). Already we have seen more bespoke forms of principal preparation (Crawford and Earley, 2010) and a recognition that 'one size does not fit all'. This must be seen as the best way forward and a good use of limited resources.

Concluding note – of pessimism and optimism!

More and more countries are moving towards decentralization, schools are more autonomous in their decision making, and increasingly held to account for their results which are made public and widely available. As schools have gained more autonomy, the more important the role of school leaders, especially the headteacher, has become. However, for Cranston (2013), 'the rhetoric of self-management and devolution across some decades now has not resulted in schools and school leaders (that is the professionals) determining and driving educational priorities' (p. 131) and many school leaders have become the 'doers' of the bidding of others rather than 'playing a lead role in shaping school leadership professionalism and education more broadly for the 21st century' (p. 132).

The research on the leadership landscape in England (2012) reported that the majority of school leaders viewed the move towards greater autonomy in positive terms, however, realistically they did not anticipate gaining further autonomy in practice. A greater proportion of heads could be defined as 'confident' than 'concerned' but the 2012 study identified some worrying trends: how a combination of increasing site-level responsibilities, diminishing support from LAs and differential regulation of schools, largely through the inspection process, may be leading to the intensification of existing hierarchies between schools. Some developments, such as the growth of Teaching Schools and their alliances may leave a significant number of schools, up to half according to some calculations, outside of any partnership or collaborative arrangements. The situation of primary schools is of particular concern and their lack of capacity to work in partnerships raises 'the spectre of the two-tier system, with some schools collaborating and improving while others – for reasons of will, capacity or simple geography – fall by the wayside' (NC, 2013, p. 13). There is a real danger that the gap between the outstanding and good schools and the rest could widen to the detriment of the education system as a whole. Some school leaders will 'embrace partnerships and a more autonomous role in driving improvement and others shy away from it, for different, often valid reasons' (NC, 2013, p. 6).

Research has consistently shown that leadership matters and the roles of school leaders, especially principals and headteachers, are not going to diminish in importance during the remainder of this century. Yet leaders need to be enabled to concentrate their professional efforts on leading the learning and the challenge for governments and policy makers is to make the work of school leaders do-able, not harder and less attractive.

In the words of an English primary head:

> The headship bar is already set at a level where only the very best, most resilient heads can attempt to clear it . . . we need to bring the job of headship within the reach of a normal human being with fire and passion for education and a modicum of organisational ability. This will not only benefit heads, but more importantly our children. (Byrne, 2006, p. 26)

Is this view still accurate today? Probably so, but there is evidence that headship is regarded as immensely rewarding. As Robert Hill remarked:

> Being a school leader is both a privilege and a demanding challenge. To have the responsibility for helping to shape young lives is a high calling. But it can become an all-consuming and exhausting passion. It is a role that brings immense satisfaction but at times great frustration. Sustaining the vision, the energy and the enthusiasm can be hard. (Hill, 2006, p. 101)

But is it fair to expect people to do such a high-powered and demanding job for a number of years and to continue to do it well? Is it surprising that there continue to be recruitment and retention difficulties over the time-period of this book (Howson, 2012)? Is headship the attraction that it once was? If headship is to be seen as attractive and manageable, then consideration must be given to reducing the demands of the job and providing more assistance, support and development with the recognition of the need for periods of professional refreshment and rejuvenation, such as regular sabbaticals. Stroud (2006) comments that heads want three things: non-judgmental relationships; 'permission to find the job difficult'; and time put aside for their own professional development.

Education continues to go through a period of considerable change; experience and evidence suggests that over the last decade or so this is a permanent state of affairs. The National College at a high-level seminar put it like this:

> Some leaders are fearful and feel exposed; some aspirant leaders are rethinking whether to go for leadership now. But for others, this is an exciting time; they are optimistic about the future and have a growing sense of confidence in their own ability to take charge. Greater accountability

is now on the agenda but there is more emphasis on this accountability being assumed collectively. (NC, 2013, p. 5)

Optimism is key and sustaining the vision and maintaining high levels of enthusiasm and positivity can indeed be hard in the constantly changing educational landscape. But it is also what makes school leadership exciting and for many, headship continues to be the 'best job in education'. Whether this remains the case is the challenge to be faced.

References

Academies Commission (2013) *Unleashing Greatness: Getting the best from an academised system. The Report of the Academies Commission*. London: RSA/Pearson.

Baker, M. (2010) Policy changes in education speed ahead. Available at: www.guardian.co.uk/education/2010/jul/20/education-policy-changes. Accessed on: 13 August 2012.

Balarin, M., Brammer, S., James, C. and McCormack, M. (2008) *The School Governance Study*. London: Business in the Community.

Ball, S. (2011) A new research agenda for educational leadership and policy. *Management in Education*, 25(2), 50–52.

—(2009) Academies in context: Politics, business and philanthropy and heterarchical governance. *Management in Education*, 23(3), 100–3.

Ball, S., Maguire, M. and Braun, A. (2012) *How Schools Do Policy: Policy Enactment in the Secondary School*. London: Routledge.

Barber, M., Wheeler, F. and Clark, M. (2010) *Capturing the Leadership Premium: How the World's Top Systems Are Building Leadership Capacity for the Future*. London: McKinsey Corporation.

Blair, T. (2005) Independent state schools. Speech at 10 Downing Street, London. 24 October 2005.

BMG (2012) *Annual Survey 2012 Schools*. Birmingham, BMG Research. Nottingham: National College for School Leadership.

Branch, G., Hanushek, E. and Rivkin. S. (2013) School leaders matter. *Education Next*, Winter, 63–9.

Bristow, M., Ireson, G. and Coleman, A. (2007) *a Life in the Day of a Headteacher: A Study of Practice and Wellbeing*. Nottingham: National College for School Leadership.

Bruggenate, G., Luyten, H., Scheerens, J. and Sueges, P. (2012) Modeling the influence of school leadership on student attainment: How can school leaders make a difference? *Educational Administration Quarterly*, 48(1), x–y.

Brundrett, M. (1999) The national professional qualification for headship: Perceptions of the providers of taught higher degrees in educational management in England and Wales. *School Leadership and Management*, 19(4), 497–510.

Bubb, S. and Earley, P. (2010) *Helping Staff Develop in Schools*. London: Sage.

—(2007) *Leading and Managing Continuing Professional Development* (2nd edn). London: Sage.

—(2004) *Managing Teacher Workload: Work-life Balance and Wellbeing*. London: Sage.

Burkhauser, S., Gates, S., Hamilton, L. and Ikemoto, G. (2012) *First Year Principals in Urban School Districts*. New York: Rand Corporation.

Bush, T. (2008) From management to leadership: Semantic or meaningful change. *Educational Management, Administration and Leadership*, 36(2), 271–88.

Byrne, C. (2006) Mere mortals cannot steer our headship. *Times Educational Supplement*, 17 March, 26.

Caldwell, B. and Spinks, J. (1992) *Leading the Self-managing School*. London: Falmer.

Chapman, C. and Hadfield, M. (2009) Supporting the middle tier to engage with school-based networks: Change strategies for influencing and cohering. *Journal of Educational Change*, 11(3), 221–40.

Chapman, C. and Harris, A. (2004) Improving schools in difficult and challenging contexts: Strategies for improvement. *Educational Research*, 46(3), 219–28.

Chitty, C. (2011) A massive power grab from local communities: The real significance of the 2010 White Paper and the 2011 Education Bill. *FORUM*, 53(1), 11–14.

Clarke, S., Wildy, H. and Styles, I. (2011) Fit for purpose? Western Australian insights into the efficacy of principal preparation. *Journal of Educational Administration*, 49(2), 166–78.

Collins, J. (2001) *From Good to Great*. London: Random House.

Cranston, N. (2013) School leaders leading: Professional responsibility not accountability as the key focus. *Educational Management, Administration & Leadership,* 41(2), 129–42.

Crawford, M. and Earley, P. (2011) Personalised leadership development? Lessons from the pilot NPQH in England. *Educational Review*, 63(1), 105–19.

Crawford, R. and Phillips, D. (2012) Local government spending: Where is the axe falling? In C. Emmerson, P. Johnson and H. Miller (eds), *The IFS Green Budget: February 2012*. London: The Institute for Fiscal Studies, pp. 124–41.

Creese, M. and Earley, P. (1999) *Improving Schools and Governing Bodies: Making a Difference*. London: Routledge.

Cribb, A. and Gewirtz, S. (2007) Unpacking autonomy and control in education: Some conceptual and normative groundwork for a comparative analysis. *European Educational Research Journal*, 6(3): 203–13.

Curtis, A., Exley, S., Sasia, A., Sarah, T. and Whitty, G. (2008) *The Academies Programme: Progress, Problems and Possibilities*. Sutton Trust report.

Darling Hammond, L. Meyerson, D., LaPointe, A. and Orr, M. (2009) *Preparing Principals for a Changing World: Lessons from Effective School Leadership Programs*. New York: John Wiley.

Davies, B. and Davies, B. (2011) *Talent Management in Education*. London: Sage.

Day, C., Sammons, P., Hopkins, D., Harris, A., Leithwood, K., Gu, Q., Brown, E., Ahtaridou, E. and Kington, A. (2009) *The Impact of School Leadership on Pupil Outcomes: Final Report*. Nottingham: Department for Education.

Day, C., Sammons, P., Leithwood, K., Hopkins, D., Gu, Q., Brown, E. and Ahtaridou, E. (2011) *Successful School Leadership: Linking with Learning*. Maidenhead: Open University Press.

Deakin, G., James, N., Tickner, M. and Tidswell, J. (2010) *Teachers' Workload Diary Survey 2010*, DfE RR057. London: DfE.

Dean, C., Dyson, A., Gallanaugh, F., Howes, A. and Raffo, C. (2007) *School, Governors and Disadvantage*. York: Joseph Rowntree Foundation.

Department for Education (2011) *a Profile of Teachers in England from the 2010 School Workforce Census.* Research Report DFE-RR151.

—(2010a) *The Importance of Teaching: The Schools' White Paper 2010.* London: TSO.

—(2010b) *Statistical First Release: Outcomes for Children Looked After by Local Authorities in England, as at 31 March 2010.* London: Office of National Statistics.

Department for Education and Employment (1998) *National Standards for Headteachers.* Nottingham: DfEE.

Department for Education and Skills (2004) *National Standards for Headteachers.* London: DfES.

Earley, P. (2012) Observation methods: Learning about leadership practice through shadowing. *Journal of Educational, Cultural and Psychological Studies,* 6 (December), 15–31.

—(2003) Leaders or followers? Governing bodies and their role in school leadership. *Educational Management and Administration,* 31(4): 353–68.

Earley, P. and Bubb, S. (2013) A day in the life of new headteachers: Learning from observation. *Educational Management, Administration and Leadership,* 42(3), x–y.

Earley, P. and Evans, J. (2004) Making a difference? Leadership development for headteachers and deputies: Ascertaining the impact of the National College for School Leadership. *Educational Management, Administration and Leadership,* 32(3), 325–38.

Earley, P., Evans, J., Collarbone, P., Gold, A. and Halpin, D. (2002) *Establishing the Current State of School Leadership in England.* Department of Education and Skills Research Report RR336. London: HMSO.

Earley, P., Higham, R., Allen, R., Allen, T., Howson, J., Nelson, R., Rawar, S., Lynch, S., Morton, L., Mehta, P. and Sims, D. (2012) *Review of the School Leadership Landscape.* Nottingham: National College for School Leadership.

Earley, P. and Jones, J. (2010) *Accelerated Leadership Development: Fast-tracking School Leaders.* London: Institute of Education, Bedford Way series.

—(2009) Leadership development in schools. In B. Davies (ed.) *The Essentials of School Leadership* (2nd edn). London: Sage.

Earley, P., Nelson, R., Higham, R., Bubb, S., Porritt, V. and Coates, M. (2011) *Experiences of New Headteachers in Cities.* Nottingham: NCSL.

Earley, P. and Weindling, D. (2006) Consultant leaders: A new role for headteachers? *School Leadership and Management,* 26(1), 37–53.

—(2004) *Understanding School Leadership.* London: Paul Chapman/Sage.

Fink, D. (2010) *The Succession Challenge: Building and Sustaining Leadership Capacity through Succession Management.* London: Sage.

Forrester, G. and Gunter, H. (2009) School leaders: Meeting the challenge of change. In C. Chapman, and H. Gunter (eds), *Radical Reforms: Perspectives on an Era of Educational Change.* Abingdon, Oxon: Routledge.

Gabarro, J. (1987) *Dynamics of Taking Charge.* Harvard: Harvard Business School Press.

Gewirtz, S. (2002) *The Managerial School: Post-welfarism and Social Justice in Education.* London: Routledge.

Glatter, R. (2012) Persistent preoccupations: The rise and rise of school autonomy and accountability in England. *Educational Management, Administration and Leadership,* 40(5): 559–75.

Gold, A., Evans, J., Earley, P., Halpin, D. and Collarbone, P. (2003) Principled principals? Values-driven leadership: Evidence from ten cases. *Educational Management, Adminstration and Leadership,* 31(2), 127–38.

Gove, M. (2012) Speech to the freedom and autonomy for schools – National Association. 5 July 2012.

Hallinger, P. (2012) Leadership for 21st Century schools: From instructional leadership to leadership for learning. Presentation to Italian Ministry of Education, December.

Hallinger, P. and Heck, R. H. (2010) Collaborative leadership and school improvement: Understanding the impact on school capacity and student learning. *School Leadership and Management,* 30(2), 95–110.

—(2003) Understanding the contribution of leadership to school improvement. In M. Wallace and L. Poulson (eds), *Learning to Read Critically in Educational Leadership and Management.* London: Sage.

Hargreaves, D. H. (2012) *a Self-improving School System: Towards Maturity.* Nottingham: National College for School Leadership.

—(2011) *Leading a Self-improving School System.* Nottingham: National College for School Leadership.

—(2010) *Creating a Self-improving School System.* Nottingham: National College for School Leadership.

Hartley, D. (2007) The emergence of distributed leadership in education: Why now? *British Journal of Educational Studies,* 55(2), 202–14.

Hastings, A., Bramley, G., Bailey, N. and Watkins, D. (2012) *Serving Deprived Communities in a Recession.* York: Joseph Rowntree Foundation.

Helgoy, I., Homme, A. and Gewirtz, S. (2007) Local autonomy or state control? Exploring the effects of new forms of regulation in education. *European Educational Research Journal,* 6(3), 198–202.

Higham, R., Hopkins, D. and Matthews, P. (2009) *System Leadership in Practice.* Milton Keynes: Open University Press.

Hill, R. (2012) *The Missing Middle: The Case for School Commissioners.* London: Royal Society of Arts.

—(2006) *Leadership That Lasts: Sustainable School Leadership in the 21st Century.* Leicester: ASCL.

Hill, R., Dunford, J., Parish, N., Rea, S. and Sandals, L. (2012) *The Growth of Academy Chains: Implications for Leaders and Leadership.* Nottingham: National College for School Leadership.

Hill, R. and Matthews, P. (2010) *Schools Leading Schools ii: The Growing Impact of National Leaders of Education.* Nottingham: National College for School Leadership.

—(2008) *Schools leading schools: The power and potential of National Leaders of Education.* Nottingham: National College for School Leadership.

Howson, J. (2012) *Annual Survey of Senior Staff Appointments in Schools across England and Wales.* London: TSL/EDS.

—(2011) *Annual Survey of Senior Staff Appointments in Schools across England and Wales.* London: TSL/EDS.

—(2010) *Annual Survey of Senior Staff Appointments in Schools across England and Wales.* London: TSL/EDS.

Hoyle, E. and Wallace, M. (2007) Educational reform: An ironic perspective. *Educational Management, Administration and Leadership,* 35(1), 9–25.

Huber, S. (ed.) (2010) *School Leadership: International Perspectives*. Utrecht: Springer.

—(2004) *Preparing School Leaders for the 21st Century: An International Comparison of Development Programs in 15 Countries*. London: RoutledgeFalmer.

Hughes, M. (1976) The professional as administrator: The case of the secondary school head. In R. Peters (ed.), *The Role of the Head*. London: Routledge & Kegan Paul, pp. 50–62.

Hutchings, M., Seeds, K., Coleman, N., Harding, C., Mansaray, A., Maylor, U., Minty, S. and Pickering, E. (2009) *Aspects of School Workforce Remodelling*. Research Report 153. Nottingham: DCSF.

ICM (2009) *Headship Index: September to October 2009*. Report prepared for National College for School Leadership.

James, C., Brammer, S. Connolly, M., Fertig, M., James, J. and Jones, J. (2011) *The 'Hidden Givers': A Study of School Governing Bodies in England*. Berkshire: CfBT Education Trust.

James. C. (2011) *The Role of the Chair of the School Governing Body: Emerging Findings from Current Research*. Berkshire: CfBT Education Trust.

Kruger, M. and Scheerens, J. (2012) Conceptual perspectives on school leadership, Chpt 1. In J. Scheerens (ed.), *School Leadership Effects Revisited: Review and Meta-analysis of Empirical Studies*. London: Springer.

Leithwood, K., Louis, K.S., Anderson, S. and Wahlstrom, K. (2004) *How Leadership Influences Student Learning*. New York: Wallace Foundation.

Leithwood, K. and Seashore-Louis, K. (2012) *Linking Leadership to Student Learning*. San Francisco, CA: Jossey-Bass.

Levin, B. (2013) *Confident School Leadership: A Canadian Perspective*. Nottingham: National College for School Leadership.

—(2012) *System-wide Improvement in Education*. Education Policy Series 13, Paris: International Academy of Education/Unesco.

Lewis, P. and Murphy, R. (2008) New directions in school leadership. *School Leadership and Management*, 28(2), 127–46.

Lightman, B. (2013) ASCL annual conference speech. Available at: www.ascl.org.uk/events/documents/Brian-Lightman. Accessed on: 22 March 2013.

—(2011) The political agenda and key government policies. Available at: www.ascl.org.uk/events/documents/regional_information_conferences/Brian-Lightman-political-agenda-and-key-government-policies. Accessed on: 1 December 2012.

Lundquist, L. (1987) *Implementation Steering: An Actor-Structure Approach*. Lund: Studentlitterature.

MacBeath, J. (2011) No lack of principles: Leadership development in England and Scotland. *School Leadership and Management*, 31(2), 105–22.

MacBeath, J., Gronn, P., Opfer, D., Lowden, K., Fords, C., Cowie, M. and O'Brien, J. (2009) *The Recruitment and Retention of Headteachers in Scotland*. Edinburgh: Scottish Government.

MacBeath, J., O'Brien, J. and Gronn, P. (2012) Drowning or waving? Coping strategies among Scottish head teachers. *School Leadership and Management,* 32(5), 421–38.

Mansell, W. (2011) Schools cash in on academy status. *The Guardian*, Tuesday 26 April 2011. Available at: www.guardian.co.uk/education/2011/apr/26/academies-lacseg-funding-bonus-schools. Accessed on: 5 January 2013.

Matthews, P., Higham, R., Stoll, L., Brennan, J. and Riley, K. (2011) *Prepared to Lead: How Schools, Federations and Chains Grow Education Leaders.* Nottingham: National College for School Leadership.

McNamara, O., Howson, J., Gunter, H. and Fryers, A. (2010) *No Job for a Woman? The Impact of Gender in School Leadership.* Report for NASUWT.

—(2009) *The Leadership Aspirations and Careers of Black and Minority Ethnic Teachers.* Report for NASUWT and National College for Leadership of Schools and Children's Services.

National College for School Leadership (2013) *School Leadership for a Self-improving System.* Nottingham: National College for School Leadership.

—(2012) *The Shape of the School Landscape: A Seminar.* Nottingham: National College for School Leadership.

—(2011) *The Changing Role and Influence of Senior Support Staff in Schools.* Nottingham: National College for School Leadership.

—(2010) *Executive Heads.* Nottingham: National College for School Leadership.

—(2009) *School Leadership Today.* Nottingham: National College for School Leadership.

—(2007a) *What We Know about School Leadership.* Nottingham: National College for School Leadership.

—(2007b) *Greenhouse Schools: Lessons from Schools That Grow Their Own Leaders.* Nottingham: National College for School Leadership.

—(2006a) *Leadership Succession: An Overview Securing the Next Generation of School Leaders.* Nottingham: National College for School Leadership.

—(2006b) *System Leadership in Action.* Nottingham: National College for School Leadership.

OECD (2011) *Viewing the United Kingdom School System through the Prism of PISA.* Paris: OECD.

—(2009) *Improving School Leadership: The Toolkit.* Paris: OECD.

Ofsted (2012a) *The Annual Report of Her Majesty's Chief Inspector of Education, Children's Services and Skills 2010/11.* London: Ofsted.

—(2012b) *The Inspection Framework.* London: Ofsted.

—(2011a) *School Governance: Learning from the Best.* London: Ofsted.

—(2011b) *System Leadership.* London: Ofsted.

—(2010a) *The Annual Report of Her Majesty's Chief Inspector of Education, Children's Services and Skills 2009/10.* London: Ofsted.

—(2010b) *Workforce Reform in Schools: Has It Made a Difference? An Evaluation of Changes Made to the School Workforce 2003–2009.* London: Ofsted.

Ozga, J. (2009) Governing education through data in England: From regulation to self-evaluation. *Journal of Education Policy,* 24(2), 149–63.

Pont, B., Nusche, D. and Moorman, H. (2008) *Improving School Leadership, Volume 1: Policy and Practice.* Paris: OECD.

PricewaterhouseCoopers (2007) *Independent Study into School Leadership.* Department of Education and Skills, Research Report RR818A. London: HMSO.

Ranson, S. (2008) The changing governance of education. *Educational Management Administration and Leadership,* 36(2), 201–19.

Ranson, S., Farrell, C., Peim, N., Smith, P. (2005) Does governance matter for school improvement? *School Effectiveness and School Improvement,* 16(3), 305–25.

Robertson, J. and Timperley, H. (eds) (2011) *Leadership and Learning*. London: Sage.

Robinson, V. (2011) *Student-centred Leadership*. San Francisco: Jossey Bass.

Robinson, V., Hohepa, M. and Lloyd, D. (2009) *School Leadership and Student Outcomes: Identifying What Works and Why: Best Evidence Synthesis*. Wellington, New Zealand: Ministry of Education.

Ross, A. (2003) *Ethnic Minority Teachers in the Teaching Workforce*. Institute of Policy Studies Occasional Paper, London Metropolitan University.

Russell, S., Simkins, T. and Fidler, B. (1997) Overview. In B. Fidler, S. Russell and T. Simkins (eds), *Choices for Self-managing Schools: Autonomy and Accountability*. London: PCP.

Sammons, P., Taggart, B., Siraj-Blatchford, I., Sylva, K., Melhuish. E. and Barreau, S. (2006) *Variations in Teachers and Pupil Behaviours in Year 5 Classes*. DoE Research Brief No: RB817.

Scanlon, M., Earley, P. and Evans, J. (1999) *Improving the Effectiveness of School Governing Bodies*. London: DfEE.

Scheerens, J. (ed.) (2012) *School Leadership Effects Revisited: Review and Meta-analysis of Empirical Studies*. Utrecht: Springer.

Schleicher, A. (ed.) (2012) *Preparing Teachers and Developing School Leaders for the 21st Century: Lessons from Around the World*. Paris: OECD Publishing.

Simkins, T. (2012) Understanding school leadership and management development in England: Retrospect and prospect. *Educational Management, Administration and Leadership*, 40(5), 621–40.

—(1997) Autonomy and Accountability. In B. Fidler, S. Russell and T. Simkins (eds), *Choices for Self-managing Schools: Autonomy and Accountability*. London: PCP.

Smith, R. (2012) *Enabling School-driven System Leadership*. Slough: NFER.

Smithers, A. and Robinson, P. (2007) *School Headship. Present and Future*. Available at: www.nut.org.uk/resources/pdf/Headsfin.pdf. Accessed on: 15 February 2007.

Southworth, G. (2011) Connecting leadership and learning. In J. Robinson and H. Timperley (eds), *Leadership and Learning*. London: Sage.

—(2009) Learning-centred leadership. In B. Davies (ed.), *The Essentials of School Leadership* (2nd edn). London: Sage.

—(2004) Learning-centred leadership. In B. Davies (ed.), *The Essentials of School Leadership*. London: Sage.

Stevens, J., Brown, J., Knibbs, S. and Smith, J. (2005) *Follow Up Research in to the State of School Leadership in England*. London: DfES.

Stoll, L. (2011) Leading professional learning communities, Chpt 8. In J. Robertson and H. Timperley (eds), *Leadership and Learning*. London: Sage.

Stoll, L. and Seashore Louis, K. (2007) *Professional Learning Communities: Divergence, Depth and Dilemmas*. Maidenhead: McGraw-Hill International.

Stroud, V. (2006) Sustaining skills in headship: Professional development for experienced headteachers. *Educational Management, Administration and Leadership*, 34(1), 89–103.

Swaffield, S. and MacBeath, J. (2009) Leadership for learning. In J. MacBeath and N. Dempster (eds), *Connecting Leadership and Learning: Principles for Practice*. London: Routledge.

Walker, A. and Dimmock, C. (2008) Preparing leaders, preparing learners: The Hong Kong experience. In M. Brundrett and M. Crawford (eds), *Developing School Leaders: An International Perspective*. London: Routledge.

Wallace, M., Tomlinson, M. and O'Reilly, D. (2011) The mediation of acculturation: Orchestrating school leadership development in England. *Educational Management, Administration and Leadership*. 39(3), 261–82.

Waslander, S., Pater, C. and van der Weide, M. (2010) *Markets in Education: An Analytical Review of Empirical Research on Market Mechanisms in Education*. Paris: OECD.

Weindling, D. and Earley, P. (1987) *Secondary Headship: The First Years*. Windsor: NFER-Nelson.

West-Burnham, J. (2009) *Developing Outstanding Leaders: Professional Life Histories of Outstanding Headteachers*. Nottingham: National College for School Leadership.

West-Burnham, J. and Coates, M. (eds) (2005) *Personalizing Learning: Transforming Education for Every Child*. Stafford: Network Educational Press.

Whitty, G. (2008) Twenty years of progress: English education policy 1988 to the present. *Educational Management, Administration and Leadership*, 36(2), 165–84.

—(1997) Creating a quasi-market in education. In M. Apple (ed.), *Review of Research in Education*. Washington, DC: American Educational Research Association.

Wiliam, D. (2009) Changing Classroom Practice. *Education Leadership*, 65(4), 36–42.

Wylie, C. (2007) *School Governance in New Zealand: How Is It Working?* Wellington: New Zealand Council for Educational Research.

Index